Welcome to Nanette's
Country Kitchen

Welcome to Nanette's Country Kitchen

125 OF MY FAVORITE RECIPES-A COLLECTION OF ORIGINAL AND SHARED RECIPES FROM FAMILY AND FRIENDS OVER THE YEARS.

NANETTE HAGAN

Copyright © 2012 by Nanette Hagan.

Library of Congress Control Number: 2012915906
ISBN:
            Hardcover   978-1-4797-0818-5
            Softcover   978-1-4797-0817-8
            Ebook   978-1-4797-0819-2

All rights reserved. No part of this book may be reproduced or transmitted in any form or by any means, electronic or mechanical, including photocopying, recording, or by any information storage and retrieval system, without permission in writing from the copyright owner.

This book was printed in the United States of America.

To order additional copies of this book, contact:
Xlibris Corporation
1-888-795-4274
www.Xlibris.com
Orders@Xlibris.com
119043

-THANK YOU-

My Daughters- Gabrielle & Bekah, for forcing me to create ways to hide vegetables in food. I am so proud of the women you have become. I love you. ♡♡

Family & friends for sharing recipes- especially Tammy, Tim, Jennifer, Mom & Grandma Lemon, and the Hagan family for allowing me to experiment with food. You were such good sports as you "suffered" through it.

God- for giving me the desire & ability to create good food.

My Husband Karl- for eating everything and not remembering the occasional yucky combination or burned food. Thanks for encouraging me to be who I am & to share that in this cookbook. I love you more than I can ever express. ♡♡

Thank you for purchasing this cookbook. Please feel free to experiment with the recipes and adapt them to your preferences. After preparing one of my recipes it would make me very happy if someone told you that you are an amazing cook. Just smile and take all the credit. Enjoy !

There are many amazing "foodie" websites. I have found great recipes on sites like AllRecipes.com and the-girl-who-ate-everything.com- many of which I have adapted to our preferences.

Contents

1. Appetizers 9
2. Salads And Soups 21
3. Breads 39
4. Side Dishes and Veggies 53
5. Main Dishes 65
6. Cakes, Bars, Brownies and Cookies 99
7. Pies and Desserts 119
8. Drinks 145
9. Miscellaneous 153

APPETIZERS

(Pictured: (Above) Vegetable Pizza pg 18,

(Below) Cheddar Ham Spread pg 13, Cheese Crisps pg 14)

BBQ Chestnuts Easy!

This makes a large baking pan full. These are great as appetizers, just don't count on any leftovers. Gabrielle's favorite.

1 package of bacon
1 bottle of BBQ sauce- or homemade
3 cans whole water chestnuts, drained
Toothpicks

Cut the package of bacon into thirds. Wrap 1/3rd slice of bacon around a chestnut and hold in place with a toothpick. Place in a cookie sheet. Continue this process until all the bacon and chestnuts are used. Bake at 400°F for 20 minutes or until the bacon starts to look crisp. Pour the BBQ sauce into a bowl and dip each chestnut into the sauce and then place in a 9"x13" baking pan. Bake an additional 15-20 minutes or until the sauce is baked on the chestnut. Serve warm.

Baked Cinnamon Brie Tart with Apple Pecan Sauce

Makes 4 servings.

1 package refrigerated crescent roll dough
1 lb round of brie cheese- skin removed
1 Tbsp brown sugar
1 tsp cinnamon

Sauce:
3 apples, peeled, cored and diced
1/3 cup packed brown sugar
1 tsp cinnamon
¼ cup chopped pecan pieces
1/2 cup apple juice or gingerale
1 Tbsp butter

Heat oven to 375°F. Unroll the dough and flatten onto a baking sheet to make a 9" square, sealing perforations. Lay brie round in the middle of the dough. Sprinkle 1 Tbsp brown sugar and 1 tsp cinnamon on brie. Carefully bring up the sides of the dough and pinch together to seal, making sure brie is completely enclosed. Bake for 15 minutes or until the tart is golden brown. In a saucepan, combine the sauce ingredients and cook for 20-30 minutes stirring often, until sauce thickens and apples are tender. Serve sauce on top of warm brie tart or on the side.

If you can't feed a hundred people, then just feed one. - Mother Teresa

Baked Cream Cheese Appetizer

Makes 8 servings.

1 package refrigerated crescent roll dough
8oz cream cheese, softened
½ tsp dill weed
¼ tsp garlic powder
¼ tsp Cajun Seasoned salt
1 egg yolk, beaten

Heat oven to 350°F. Unroll the dough, press together seams to form a 12" x 4" rectangle. In a small bowl, combine the spices. Sprinkle half of the spices on one side of the cream cheese. Place spice-side down in the center of the dough. Sprinkle the rest of the spices on cream cheese. Enclose the cream cheese in the dough by bringing the sides together, pressing edges to seal. Place on a lightly greased baking sheet. Brush with beaten egg yolk. Bake for 15-18 minutes or until lightly browned. Serve with crackers and apple slices if desired.

Cheddar Ham Spread

Easy!

Makes 2 cups.

2 (5oz) cans chunk ham, drained (or diced, leftover ham)
¾ cup shredded cheddar cheese
½ cup mayonnaise
¼ cup sweet pickle relish
2 Tbsp minced onion

In a bowl, combine all ingredients. Cover and chill overnight or until ready to serve. Serve with assorted crackers, Cheese Crisps or on bread as a sandwich.

Cheese Crisps — Easy!

Makes about 2 dozen Crisps.

---

1 recipe for single pie crust or premade.
1 cup shredded cheese, desired flavor- I like sharp cheddar for this.
10 shakes of hot pepper sauce
Sesame seeds or poppy seeds
Course salt or parmesan cheese or Kroger Hickory Bacon salt

Heat oven to 450°F. On a lightly floured surface, knead the pie crust with the hot pepper sauce and cheese until combined. Roll out to 1/8" thickness. Cut shapes out of dough with cookie cutters and place on a baking sheet. Brush tops with water (or melted butter) and sprinkle with sesame or poppy seeds, course salt or parmesan cheese. Bake for 5-8 minutes or until golden brown.

Cheese Fondue **Easy!** Makes 6-8 servings.

4 slices of bacon
2 Tbsp minced onion
2 tsp flour
1 lb Velveeta cheese
2 cups sour cream
1 tsp Worcestershire sauce

In a saucepan, fry bacon until crisp. Drain, reserving 1 Tbsp drippings. Stir flour into drippings. Add remaining ingredients. Cook over low heat, stirring constantly until cheese is melted. Pour into a fondue pot. Top with crumbled bacon. Serve hot.

Dippers: Bread cubes, sliced vegetables, cooked meats, mushrooms, cooked tater tots, bread sticks, apple slices, etc.

Parmesan Rounds

Easy!

Makes 10-12 servings.

Premade square cocktail bread- found in most Deli's- or Italian bread
8 oz cream cheese, softened
1/4 cup butter, melted
1/8 cup + 1 Tbsp mayonnaise
3 green onions, chopped
Freshly grated parmesan cheese
Additional butter for toasting

Lightly butter 1 side of each bread slice. Broil until lightly toasted. Turn and toast other side of bread. Let cool. In a bowl, combine cream cheese, melted butter, mayonnaise and onion. Spread 1 Tbsp mixture onto buttered side of toasted bread. Dip into parmesan cheese so that the cheese sticks to the cream cheese mixture. Place on a baking sheet and broil until bubbly and golden, about 5 minutes. Serve immediately.

Ranch Pretzels

Easy!

Makes 12 cups.

1 package (16-20oz) pretzels- any shape
1 envelope ranch salad dressing mix
¾ cup vegetable oil
1-1/2 tsp dill weed
1-1/2 tsp garlic powder

Combine all ingredients, add pretzels, stir to coat. Pour onto an ungreased 15"x10" baking pan. Bake at 200°F for 1 hour, stirring every 15 minutes. Let cool.

Vegetable Pizza

Makes 6-8 servings.

This is good as an appetizer or side dish. Nice summertime treat.

8oz cream cheese, softened
1/4 cup green onion, chopped
1/4 cup mayonnaise
1 tsp horseradish sauce
1/8 tsp hot pepper sauce
Sliced and chopped raw vegetables
1-1/2 cup shredded cheese- optional
1 pie crust, rolled out onto a pizza pan and baked until golden brown, cooled

In a mixing bowl, combine the first 5 ingredients, mixing well. Spread onto the cooled pie crust. Arrange the sliced and chopped vegetables on the cream cheese mixture. Sprinkle shredded cheese on top if desired. Chill until ready to serve. Use a pizza cutter to cut into squares or wedges.

Options for sliced and chopped vegetables- Tomatoes, carrots, celery, radishes, zucchini, mushrooms, broccoli, cauliflower, peas, onions. Any vegetable that you enjoy raw could go on this pizza.

Variations- Use refrigerated crescent roll dough instead of pie crust as the base for this pizza. Spread out on a pizza pan and bake as directed until golden brown. Cool.

Your life is an occasion. Rise to it! (Unknown)

Vegetable Sticks

Makes 2 dozen.

---

3 medium carrots
6 fresh asparagus spears
6 broccoli spears
11oz tube refrigerated breadsticks
1 egg white, lightly beaten
¼ cup grated parmesan cheese
½ tsp seasoned salt or BBQ seasoning

Heat oven to 375°F. Cut carrots lengthwise into quarters. In a large pan, place carrots in boiling water, cook 3 minutes. Add asparagus and broccoli, cook 3 minutes longer. Drain and rinse with cold water. Dry completely. Cut each breadstick in half. Wrap each breadstick around each vegetable. Place on a lightly greased baking pan with breadstick ends down. Combine parmesan cheese and seasoning. Brush breadstick with egg white. Sprinkle with cheese mixture. Bake 12-14 minutes or until golden brown. Serve warm.

SALADS AND SOUPS

(Pictured: Chicken Salad pg 23, Potato Salad pg 28,
Pea- Cheese Salad pg 27, Microwave Pickles pg 157)

Tip- Most salads are better if made a day ahead so flavors have a chance to develop.

Broccoli Salad

Makes 8 servings.

Karl's Favorite 💕 Thanks for the recipe June-Bug.

1 bunch broccoli florets- washed & dried thoroughly (6 cups bite-sized pieces)
1 small onion- optional
½ cup sunflower seeds
1 cup grapes, washed & dried thoroughly, quartered
6 slices of bacon- fried, drained and crumbled
1 cup mayonnaise
½ cup sugar
2 tsp vinegar

In a large bowl, combine the broccoli, onion, sunflower seeds and grapes. In a small bowl, combine the mayonnaise, sugar and vinegar. Pour over broccoli mixture and stir well. Sprinkle bacon crumbles on top. Cover and refrigerate overnight. Stir well before serving.

Chicken Salad

This will make 10-12 servings.

2 cups grapes- washed, dried and chopped
1 cup chopped celery
1-1/2 cups chopped onion
1 cup sweet pickle relish
5 lbs chicken breasts
2-1/2 to 3-1/2 cups mayonnaise
1 tsp salt
½ tsp celery seed, if desired
½ cup toasted slivered almonds, if desired

Boil chicken until cooked through. While it's still hot, shred chicken with hands into a large bowl. Place grapes, celery, onion and pickle relish into a strainer and strain off juices. Add to chicken in bowl. Add salt, celery seed and slivered almonds. Stir in enough mayonnaise to make desired consistency. This is best if made the day before eating it so the flavors can blend. Serve on a toasted croissant, or on a bed of lettuce.

Oriental Chicken Salad

Makes 4-6 servings.

½ cup sugar
1 Tbsp cornstarch
¼ cup water
¼ cup vegetable oil
¼ cup ketchup
3 Tbsp cider vinegar
1 Tbsp soy sauce
1 bag of mixed salad greens
2 cups cubed, cooked chicken
1 cup salted cashew pieces
8oz sliced water chestnuts, drained
6oz snow peas
Chow Mein noodles
Chopped green onion

In a small saucepan, combine the first 7 ingredients. Bring to a boil, cook and stir 2 minutes or until thickened. Cool. In a large salad bowl combine the remaining ingredients. Pour in dressing and toss to coat. Serve immediately.

German-Style Potato Salad

Makes 6-8 servings.

---

2 lbs small new potatoes, washed
2 hard-boiled eggs, sliced
1 tsp dill weed
½ lb smoked sausage, cubed
1 onion, chopped
2 Tbsp flour
2 Tbsp sugar
¼ cup apple cider vinegar
1 can chicken broth
Dash of pepper
¼ cup sliced green olives

In a 4qt saucepan, add the potatoes adding enough water to cover. Heat to boiling. Reduce heat, cover and simmer for 20 minutes or until potatoes are fork tender. Cool slightly. Cut potatoes into slices. In a large bowl, combine potatoes, eggs and dill weed. In a skillet, fry the sausage and onion until meat is browned, stirring often. Reserve the drippings in the skillet. Drain well and spoon sausage and onion into the potato mixture. Stir flour into the drippings and cook 1 minute, stirring constantly. Add sugar, vinegar, broth and pepper. Cook until mixture boils, stirring constantly. Sauce will thicken. Pour over potato mixture, toss gently to coat. Sprinkle with olives. Serve warm.

Give a man a fish; you have fed him for today. Teach a man to fish; and you have fed him for a lifetime. - Chinese Proverb

Mom's Bean Salad   Easy!

Makes 6-8 servings.

2 cans hot chili beans, undrained
¼ cup chopped onion
¾ cup chopped dill pickles, drained
¾ cup chopped sweet pickles, drained
1/4 cup mayonnaise
½ tsp salt
2 hard-boiled eggs, cubed
1 Tbsp taco seasoning

In a large bowl, combine all ingredients until well blended. Cover and chill overnight to blend the flavors. Serve on shredded lettuce or with crackers.

Pea-Cheese Salad **Easy!** Makes 6 servings.

10oz package frozen raw peas, thawed, drained
1 cup cubed cheddar cheese
2 hard-boiled eggs, peeled and chopped
¼ cup chopped celery
2 Tbsp chopped onion
1/3 cup mayonnaise
2 Tbsp sugar
½ tsp dill weed
½ tsp salt
1/8 tsp pepper

In a bowl, combine mayonnaise, sugar, dill weed, salt and pepper. Stir in the remaining ingredients. Chill until ready to serve.

Potato Salad

Makes 8-10 Servings.

---

4 lbs potatoes, cubed, cooked, cooled
1/2 cup chopped celery
2/3 cup chopped onion
1-1/4 cups sweet relish, drained
1 cup mayonnaise
1-1/2 Tbsp sugar
1 tsp salt
1 tsp dill weed
½ tsp celery seed

In a large mixing bowl, combine all ingredients. With clean hands, stir the ingredients, squeezing some of the potatoes- this will thicken the potato salad. Chill.

NANETTE HAGAN

Spicy Ranch Salad With Chicken Makes 8-10 servings.

8oz jar salsa- hot, medium or mild as desired
12oz bottle Ranch dressing
2 cups cubed, cooked chicken
1 large bag of mixed salad greens
1-1/2 cups chopped carrots
1 cup chopped celery
½ cup chopped onion
1 cup chopped tomato
- Other chopped vegetables as desired (peppers, zucchini, mushrooms, squash, cucumbers, broccoli, cauliflower, etc.)
- Croutons, nuts, Chinese noodles, bacon bits, sunflower seeds.

In a blender, mix salsa and salad dressing. Cover and chill until ready to serve. In a large bowl, add remaining ingredients. Pour salad dressing on and toss gently. Serve immediately.

Sweet Coleslaw

Makes 8-10 servings.

---

1 medium cabbage- washed, dried and chopped
1 carrot-washed, dried and finely chopped
1 cup half & half
½ cup sugar
1/3 cup vinegar
2 Tbsp mayonnaise
¼ cup chopped onion
1 Tbsp horseradish
2 tsp salt

Place the chopped cabbage and carrot in a large bowl. In a food processor, chop the onion, add the remaining ingredients and process until smooth. Pour over the cabbage, stirring to coat. Chill overnight.

Prior to the Internet, the last technology that had any real effect on the way people sat down and talked together was the table. Clay Shirky

Bacon & Potato Soup

Makes 6 servings.

Bekah's favorite meal 💕 *Shredded cheese is good in this soup too.*

5 cups potatoes, peeled, cubed
8 slices of bacon
2 Tbsp flour
3 cups milk
1 cup beef broth
Salt and pepper to taste
1 tsp onion powder
1 Tbsp chives
1 cup sour cream or French onion dip

In an electric skillet, fry the bacon until crisp. Remove the bacon and add the potatoes to the bacon grease in the skillet. Brown the potato cubes. Sprinkle the flour over the potatoes, this will thicken up any remaining grease. Slowly stir in enough milk to cover the potatoes. Add the salt and pepper and beef broth. Cover and cook until potatoes are tender and soup has thickened, about 1 hour. Stir in the sour cream. Heat through but don't boil. Crumble the bacon and add to the soup. Serve hot.

Beef Stew With Mostaccioli

Makes 6-8 servings.

1-1/2 lb beef chuck roast, boneless
2 Tbsp vegetable or olive oil
1 envelope onion soup mix
1 tsp salt
½ tsp chili powder
2-1/2 cups water
16oz can diced tomatoes, undrained
1-1/2 tsp ketchup
¼ cup cooking sherry
2 cups carrots, sliced
½ cup celery, sliced
½ cup onion, chopped
1 cup uncooked Mostaccioli

In a Dutch oven, brown meat in oil. Add remaining ingredients except mostaccioli. Cover and simmer 2 hours or until meat is tender. Stir to shred meat. Stir in mostaccioli. Cook 15-20 minutes or until mostaccioli is tender. Serve warm.

This can also be made in a slow cooker set on low. Increase cooking time to 6-8 hours.

Easy Beef Noodle Soup Makes 6-8 servings.

1 lb ground beef
46oz can of V8 Juice
1 envelope onion soup mix.
3oz package beef ramen noodles
16oz package frozen mixed vegetables

In a large saucepan or Dutch oven, cook beef until no longer pink, drain. Stir in the V8 juice, soup mix, beef noodle seasoning packet and mixed vegetables. Bring to a boil, reduce heat and simmer, uncovered for 10 minutes or until vegetable are tender. Bring to a boil and add ramen noodles. Cook 3 minutes or until noodles are tender.

(Pictured: (Above) Easy Beef Noodle Soup pg 33, V-8 Cheese Loaves pg 51, (Below) Bacon & Potato Soup pg 31, Pizza Bread pg 49)

Chicken and Cheese Chowder

Makes 6-8 servings.

2 cups potatoes, peeled and diced
2 chicken bouillon cubes
½ cup sliced carrots
½ cup chopped celery
¼ cup chopped onion
1 can white corn, drained
1-1/2 tsp salt
¼ tsp pepper
¼ cup butter
¼ cup flour
2 cups milk
2 cups shredded cheddar cheese
2 cup cubed, cooked chicken

In a Dutch oven, dissolve bouillon in 2 cups water. Add vegetables and spices. Cover and simmer 30 minutes, do not drain. In a saucepan, melt butter, add flour and blend well. Add milk, whisking constantly. Cook over low heat, stirring often until sauce thickens. Add cheese, stirring until melted. Add sauce and chicken to Dutch oven, stirring well. Heat through but don't boil. Serve warm.

I wonder what God was thinking when he created you? He must have been thinking about me ♡

(Pictured: Tortellini & Sausage Stew pg 37, Cheesy Garlic Bread pg 41)

As the days grow short, some faces grow long. But not mine. Every autumn, when the wind turns cold and darkness comes early, I am suddenly happy. It's time to start making soup again. Leslie Newman

Tortellini and Sausage Stew

Makes 10-12 servings.

---

1 lb Italian sausage- sweet or spicy
1 cup chopped onion
4 cloves garlic, minced
10 cups beef broth or stock
½ cup water
1 cup dry red wine
2 cans (28oz each) peeled, chopped tomatoes
8oz tomato sauce
1 cup thinly sliced carrots
1 cup thinly sliced celery
1-1/2 tsp dried oregano
1-1/2 tsp dried basil
2 cups dry tortellini
3 Tbsp dried parsley

Remove casings from sausage and cut into bite-size pieces. In a Dutch oven or large pot, brown sausage. Drain all but 1 Tbsp of the fat. Sauté onions, garlic, carrots and celery in the fat. Return sausage to the pot along with the broth, water, wine, tomatoes, tomato sauce, oregano and basil. Bring to a boil. Reduce heat and simmer 30 minutes uncovered. Skim off any fat. Stir in tortellini and parsley. Simmer, uncovered, 45 minutes. Serve hot.

BREADS

(Pictured: (Above) V-8 Cheese Loaves pg 51, (Below) Pizza Bread pg 49)

Banana Bread

Makes 1 loaf.

The way to a man's heart......

1 cup sugar
1/3 cup butter, softened
2 eggs
1-1/2 cup mashed bananas
1/3 cup water
1-2/3 cups flour
1 tsp baking soda
½ tsp salt
¼ tsp baking powder
½ cup chopped nuts, optional

Heat oven to 350°F. Grease the bottom of a loaf pan. In a mixing bowl, cream sugar and butter. Mix in eggs until well blended. Add bananas and water and beat until combined. Stir in remaining ingredients until just moistened. Pour into prepared loaf pan. Bake for 60-70 minutes or until a knife inserted in the center comes out clean. This bread will be more moist if you place a pie pan filled with water on the oven rack below the bread.
Cool in the loaf pan 5-10 minutes. Remove from pan and cool on a wire rack. To keep the bread moist, store in a sealed container or zip-lock bag.

Cheesy Garlic Bread

Makes 6-8 servings.

8oz cream cheese, softened
¼ cup sour cream
¼ cup grated parmesan cheese
2 Tbsp mayonnaise
1 tsp parsley
¼ tsp garlic salt
½ tsp onion powder
1 Tbsp minced green onion
6-8 garlic cloves, minced
1 loaf (1lb) French bread, cut into 1" slices

In a mixing bowl, combine the first 9 ingredients. Beat until well blended. Spread mixture on 1 side of each slice of bread and place on an ungreased baking sheet. Broil for 3-4 minutes or until cheese mixture is bubbly and lightly browned.

Cinnamon Crescent Rolls Makes 8 rolls.

1 package of refrigerated crescent roll dough
1/4 cup butter, softened
1/2 tablespoon cinnamon
1/4 cup sugar

Heat oven to 375°F. Combine the cinnamon and sugar together and mix well. Place the unrolled crescent rolls onto an ungreased cookie sheet. Brush butter onto each triangle; top with cinnamon and sugar mixture. Roll dough from the bottom of the triangle to the point. Bake for 8-10 minutes or until golden brown. Serve warm.

Coffeecake With Cream Cheese Swirl

Makes 1 coffeecake.

6oz cream cheese, softened
2 Tbsp lemon juice
2 Tbsp powdered sugar
2 cups flour
1 tsp baking powder
1 tsp baking soda
¼ tsp salt
1 cup sugar
½ cup butter or margarine, softened
3 eggs
1 tsp vanilla extract
6oz French vanilla yogurt
2 Tbsp milk

Topping:
¼ cup finely chopped nuts
2 Tbsp sugar
½ tsp cinnamon

Heat oven to 350°F. In a mixing bowl, beat cream cheese, lemon juice and powdered sugar. Set aside. Sift together flour, baking powder, baking soda and salt. In a mixing bowl, cream butter and sugar until fluffy. Add eggs and vanilla. Mix well. Add dry ingredients alternately with yogurt, mixing well. Pour half of the batter into a greased and floured loaf pan. Spoon cream cheese mixture on top of batter, not going all the way to the edges. Mix together the topping ingredients and sprinkle half onto cream cheese mixture. Spoon remaining batter over topping, spreading all the way to the edges. Sprinkle remaining topping on batter. Bake for 45-50 minutes or until a knife inserted in the center comes out clean. Serve warm.

Grandma Lemon's Coffeecake   Makes 1 large coffeecake.

1-1/4 cups flour
¾ cup pastry flour
2/3 cup sugar
2 Tbsp baking powder
1 tsp salt
2 eggs
1 cup milk
½ cup vegetable oil
1 tsp vanilla extract

Topping:
2/3 cup brown sugar
2/3 cup flour
2/3 cup sugar
¾ tsp cinnamon
¼-1/3 cup butter, melted

Heat oven to 425°F. In a mixing bowl, combine the eggs, milk, oil and vanilla. Add dry ingredients. Mix until just combined. Pour into a greased 9"x13" baking pan. In a bowl, combine the topping ingredients until crumbly. Sprinkle on top of batter. Bake for 20 minutes or until golden brown and a knife inserted in the center comes out clean.

"Americans are just beginning to regard food the way the French always have. Dinner is not what you do in the evening before something else. Dinner is the evening." Art Buchwald

Mom's Rhubarb Bread

Makes 1 loaf.

1-1/2 cups brown sugar
2/3 cup vegetable oil
1 egg
1 cup sour milk (1 cup milk, 2 drops lemon juice)
1 tsp vanilla extract
1-1/2 cups flour
1 cup pastry flour
1 tsp baking soda
1 tsp salt
1-1/2 cups chopped rhubarb

Topping:
½ cup sugar
½ tsp cinnamon
1 Tbsp butter, melted

Heat oven to 325°F. In a mixing bowl, combine first 5 ingredients. In a bowl sift together dry ingredients. Add flour mixture to wet ingredients, mix until well blended. Stir in rhubarb. Pour batter into a greased loaf pan. Mix the sugar and cinnamon, sprinkle onto batter. Drizzle with melted butter. Bake 55-60 minutes or until a toothpick inserted in the center comes out clean. Cool

My Favorite Cornbread

Makes 1 cornbread- 6-8 servings.

1 cup cornmeal- I mix yellow and white
1 cup all-purpose flour
½ tsp baking soda
1 tsp. baking powder
1 tsp. salt
3 Tbsp sugar
6 Tbsp butter
1 cup + 2 Tbsp buttermilk
2 eggs

Heat oven to 400°F. In a bowl, combine the dry ingredients. Cut in the butter- I use my small food processor. In a bowl, combine the buttermilk and eggs. Stir in the dry ingredients until just blended. Pour into a greased 2 qt casserole dish or pie pan or greased muffin pan. Bake for 25-30 minutes (2qt) 13-16 minutes (muffins) or until a toothpick inserted near center comes out clean. Serve hot with butter and honey or maple syrup.

Makes 12 muffins.

Work like you don't need money, Love like you've never been hurt, And dance like no one's watching.—Aurora Greenway

(Pictured: (Above) My Favorite Cornbread pg 46,
(Below) Pancakes pg 48)

Pancakes Easy!

Makes 16-18 pancakes.

This recipe makes a nice, fluffy pancake. It's easy to mix up a batch of the dry ingredients to keep on hand. Just add the wet ingredients for a fast breakfast. Great for a different meal while camping too! During my years in VT, I helped with several Pancakes Breakfasts- flipping about 800 of these pancakes each time.

Basic recipe:
2 cups flour
2-1/2 tsp baking powder
1 tsp salt
1/3 cup sugar
1/3 cup vegetable oil
1-1/2 cups milk
2 eggs
1 Tbsp vanilla extract

In a bowl, stir together the oil, vanilla, milk and eggs. Stir in the flour, sugar, baking powder and salt. This should be the consistency of a milkshake. Use a ladle to spoon batter out onto a hot griddle. Brown pancakes on both sides. Serve hot.

Variations: Stir in blueberries, chopped strawberries, chocolate chips, chopped apples, cinnamon, etc.

You only live once, but if you do it right, once is enough. Mae West

Pizza Bread

Makes 1 loaf or 10 rolls.

This bread is great right out of the oven, sliced and buttered with parmesan cheese sprinkled on top, with soup or as a sandwich- like a Muffaletta.

3-1/2 oz package chopped pepperoni
3 cups flour
1 package yeast
½ tsp oregano
¼ tsp garlic powder
1-1/4 cups water
2 Tbsp butter
2 Tbsp sugar
1 tsp salt

In the microwave, heat water, butter, sugar and salt until just warm (110°F -120°F). Pour into a large bowl and add yeast, garlic powder and oregano. Stir until yeast is dissolved. Add ½ of the flour and beat for 3 minutes. Stir in remaining flour and pepperoni to combine. Let dough rise in the bowl 30 minutes. Place dough into a greased loaf pan or divide into 10 balls and place on a cookie sheet. Let dough rise in a warm place until 3 times it's original size. Bake at 375°F for 35-40 minutes (loaf) or 15-20 minutes (rolls) or until golden brown. Remove from pan, cool.

Sweet Tropical Bread

Makes 2 loaves.

These are great little treats to give away. They can be made in cupcake or small loaf pans if desired.

1 package yellow cake mix
8oz can crushed pineapple, undrained
1 cup evaporated milk
2 eggs
½ tsp ground nutmeg
½ cup flaked coconut

Glaze:
1-1/2 cups powdered sugar
2 Tbsp milk
1-2 drops coconut extract
2 Tbsp toasted coconut

Heat oven to 325°F. In a mixing bowl, combine the first 5 ingredients and beat until just combined. Stir in coconut. Pour into 2 greased loaf pans and bake for 45-50 minutes or until a toothpick inserted near center comes out clean. Cool for 10 minutes, remove from pans and cool completely. In a small bowl, combine powdered sugar, milk and coconut extract until smooth. Drizzle over the cooled loaves. Sprinkle toasted coconut on top.

"A man seldom thinks with more earnestness of anything than he does of his dinner." Samuel Johnson (1709-1784)

V-8 Cheese Loaves

Makes 2 loaves of bread.

A tasty way to hide vegetables. This bread turns out orange-colored. And it makes an awesome grilled cheese or grilled ham and cheese sandwich.

5-1/2 to 6 cups unbleached flour
2 packages active dry yeast
1-1/2 tsp salt
1 cup V-8 juice
¾ cup water
3 Tbsp butter
1-1/2 cups shredded cheddar cheese
1 egg

In a large bowl, combine 2 cups flour, yeast and salt. Set aside. In a small saucepan, heat V-8 juice, water and butter until warm (110-115°F). Pour into the flour mixture and beat for 30 seconds. Add cheese and egg and beat for 3 minutes with a mixer. Stir in 2-1/2 cups flour. Dump dough out onto a floured surface and knead until smooth and elastic, about 6 minutes, adding remaining flour while kneading. Shape dough into a ball and place in a large greased bowl, turning greased side up. Cover and let rise in a warm place until doubled in bulk, about 1 hour. Grease 2 loaf pans. Punch down the dough, divide in half. Shape into two loaves and place in loaf pans. Cover and let rise in a warm place for 45 minutes. Heat oven to 375°F. Bake loaves for 35 minutes or until golden brown and loaves sound hollow when tapped. Remove from pans. Rub the top with a little butter if desired. Cool on a wire rack.

SIDE DISHES AND VEGGIES

(Pictured: (Above) Broccoli with Morney Sauce pg 55,
(Below) Maple Glazed Carrots pg 59)

Baked Beans

Makes 6-8 servings.

This recipe came from an Amish family in Indiana. This can also be made by combining all ingredients into a crock pot and cook on low heat for 6-8 hours.

2 cans (15oz) navy or great northern beans, drained
1/2 lb bacon, fried and drained, crumbled
1-1/2 cups ketchup
3 tsp vinegar
1 medium sweet onion, chopped
3/4 cup brown sugar
¼ cup maple syrup or molasses
Salt and pepper to taste

In a Dutch oven, cook beans in enough water to cover for 30 minutes, drain. Set beans aside. In the Dutch oven, fry the bacon until crisp, drain. Remove all but 1 Tbsp grease and drippings. Fry the onions in the bacon grease until tender. Add all ingredients to the Dutch oven and stir well. Cook on low heat, covered, for 1 hour or until desired consistency, stirring often. Serve hot.

Broccoli with Morney Sauce

Makes 6-8 servings.

1 bunch of broccoli, washed and cut up
½ cup finely chopped onion
2 Tbsp butter
3 Tbsp flour
2 cups milk
1/2 cup grated Swiss cheese
½ tsp salt
1/8 tsp pepper
Dash of nutmeg
¼ cup grated parmesan cheese
¼ cup dried bread crumbs
2 Tbsp butter, melted

Cook the broccoli until crisp tender. In a saucepan, sauté onion in 2 Tbsp butter for 3 minutes. Add flour. Cook 1 minute, stirring constantly. Add milk, whisking constantly. Cook over medium heat for 5 minutes or until sauce thickens. Stir in Swiss cheese and spices. Place broccoli in a greased 2 qt baking dish. Pour the sauce over the broccoli. Combine the parmesan cheese and bread crumbs. Sprinkle on top of sauce. Drizzle melted butter on top. Bake, uncovered, at 375°F for 20-25 minutes or until lightly browned.

It's easy to make a buck. It's a lot tougher to make a difference. Tom Brokaw

Corn Pudding

Makes 8-10 servings.

When I want to see our family in Vermont, I know what to do. Make this and Maple Pecan Pork Chops and its family time! ♡

1 can whole kernel corn, drained
1 can creamed style corn
½ cup butter
1 box jiffy corn muffin mix
1 cup sour cream
2 eggs, lightly beaten
1 tsp salt

Melt butter in a 9"x13" baking pan in the oven at 375°F, turn carefully to coat bottom of pan. In a bowl, combine remaining ingredients with the melted butter. Pour back into baking pan. Bake for 35-40 minutes or until cake-like and golden brown on top. Serve warm.

Creamy Italian Noodles Makes 4-6 servings.

8 oz wide egg noodles
¼ cup margarine or butter, melted
½ cup heavy whipping cream
¼ cup grated parmesan cheese
2-1/4 tsp Italian Salad Dressing mix.

Cook noodles according to package directions, drain and place in a serving bowl. Toss with butter. Add the remaining ingredients and mix well. Serve immediately.

There are those who give with joy, and that joy is their reward.- Kahlil Gibran

Green Beans with Chestnuts & Bacon

Makes 4-5 servings.

2 strips bacon
½ cup water chestnuts, drained, chopped
2 Tbsp onion, chopped
2 cans French-style green beans, drained well
Seasoned Salt and pepper to taste

In a skillet, fry the bacon until crisp. Drain, reserving 1 Tbsp drippings. In the reserved drippings, fry onion and chestnuts. Add the green beans and stir fry 5 minutes or until heated through. Add seasoned salt and pepper. Stir in crumbled bacon.

Variation- Use cooked broccoli or cauliflower instead of green beans.

Maple Glazed Carrots **Easy!**

Makes 4 servings.

1 lb baby carrots, washed
2 Tbsp butter
½ cup maple syrup
¼ cup apple juice
½ tsp cinnamon
¼ tsp salt

Steam carrots until almost tender. In a saucepan, combine butter, maple syrup, juice, cinnamon, and salt. Cook until butter is melted. Add carrots and cook until carrots are tender and sauce has thickened, about 25-30 minutes. Serve warm.

Oven-Fried Zucchini Circles Makes 6-8 servings.

2 small zucchini, cut into ¼" slices
1 egg, beaten
½ cup bread crumbs
¼ cup Parmesan cheese
½ tsp salt or seasoned salt
½ tsp garlic pepper
½ tsp onion powder

Heat oven to 425°F. Line a baking sheet with aluminum foil and brush with olive oil. In a bowl, combine crumbs, cheese and seasonings. Dip zucchini slices in egg and then in crumbs. Place slices on the baking sheet. Bake for 10 minutes or until golden brown and crispy. Serve warm.

Saucy Potatoes

Easy!

Makes 4 servings.

---

1 can (10-3/4oz) condensed cream of chicken soup
¼ cup chicken broth
5 medium potatoes, peeled, cubed and cooked. (leftover potatoes will work)
Salt and pepper to taste
1 tsp chives
½ tsp onion powder
Parmesan cheese- if desired

In a saucepan, combine soup and broth, stir in potatoes, salt, pepper and spices. Cook over medium-low heat until mixture begins to simmer and potatoes are heated through. Sprinkle parmesan cheese on top if desired.

Savory Rice

Makes 6 servings.

This recipe is great for gifts-in-a-jar. Just pour dry ingredients into a pint-sized canning jar, add a note about how to cook it and the liquid ingredients. Attach a bow and you have a ready-made gift.

3/4 cup white rice
¾ cup brown rice
3 beef bouillon cubes, crumbled
¾ tsp rosemary
¾ tsp thyme
1 Tbsp minced onion
½ tsp onion powder
½ tsp garlic powder
3-1/2 cups water
2 Tbsp butter
Dash of Worcestershire sauce

In a saucepan combine water and butter. Bring to a boil. Add remaining ingredients. Reduce heat, cover and simmer for 20-25 minutes, or until liquid is absorbed and rice is tender.

Sweet Potato Casserole

Makes 8 servings.

This can easily pass as a dessert. It tastes a lot like pumpkin pie without the crust.

3lbs yams, drained
¼ cup butter, melted
1/4 cup milk
½ cup sugar
1 tsp vanilla extract
1 tsp cinnamon
1 tsp pumpkin pie spice
1-1/2 cups marshmallows
1 cup coconut flakes- optional

Topping:
¼ cup butter, melted
½ cup brown sugar
½ cup chopped pecans

Heat oven to 350°F. Mash the yams in a bowl with butter, milk, sugar, vanilla and spices. In a greased 2 qt casserole dish, layer the marshmallows on the bottom and up the sides. Sprinkle coconut on top if desired. Pour the yam mixture on the coconut. In a small skillet, melt the butter for the topping, stir in brown sugar and nuts. Pour topping over the yam mixture. Bake for 30-35 minutes or until hot and bubbly.

May you live all the days of your life. Jonathan Swift

Vegetable Casserole

Makes 6-8 servings.

---

1 can shoe-peg white corn, drained
2 cans French-style green beans, drained
½ cup sour cream
1 can condensed cream of celery soup
½ cup onion, chopped
1/2 sleeve Ritz crackers, crushed
1/2 cup slivered almonds, divided
1/3 cup butter, melted
1 cup shredded cheddar cheese, optional

Heat oven to 350°F. In a bowl, combine the first 5 ingredients. Add 1/4 cup almonds and ½ cup shredded cheese. Pour into a greased 2 qt casserole dish. Sprinkle ½ cup cheese on top. In a bowl, combine the cracker crumbs, 1/4 cup almonds and melted butter until crumbly. Sprinkle on top of casserole. Bake for 30 minutes or until cheese is melted and casserole is bubbly.

Eating is not merely a material pleasure. Eating well gives a spectacular joy to life and contributes immensely to goodwill and happy companionship. It is of great importance to the morale. Elsa Schiaparelli

MAIN DISHES

(Pictured: Quiche pg 88, Broccoli Salad pg 22)

(Pictured-Broccoli Ham Casserole pg 67, Creamy Italian Noodles pg 57, Banana Split Salad pg 125)

Broccoli Ham Casserole

Makes 4-6 servings.

10-12oz frozen chopped broccoli (or leftover)
¼ cup chopped onion
4 Tbsp butter, divided
2 Tbsp flour
2-1/2 cups milk
Salt and pepper to taste
½ tsp Penzeys Smoky 4/S seasoned salt
Dash of nutmeg
½ cup shredded sharp cheddar cheese
2 cups cooked, cubed ham
1-1/2 cups seasoned croutons

Heat oven to 350°F. Cook broccoli according to package directions. In a large saucepan, sauté onion in 3 Tbsp butter until tender. Stir in flour until blended, gradually add milk, whisking to prevent lumps. Stir in salt and pepper, seasoned salt and nutmeg. Bring to a boil, cook and stir for 2 minutes or until thickened. Reduce heat, stir in cheese until melted.
Drain broccoli. Add broccoli, ham and 1 cup croutons to the cheese sauce. Pour into a greased 2 qt baking dish. Melt 1 Tbsp butter, toss with remaining croutons. Sprinkle on the casserole. Bake, uncovered, for 25-30 minutes or until golden brown.

Food is so primal, so essential a part of our lives, often the mere sharing of recipes with strangers turns them into good friends. Jasmine Heiler

Cashew Chicken Casserole

Makes 6 servings.

2 cups uncooked elbow macaroni
3 cups cooked, cubed chicken
½ cup cubed processed American cheese
1 small onion, chopped
½ cup celery, chopped
1 can sliced water chestnuts, drained
1 can condensed cream of mushroom soup***
1 can condensed cream of chicken soup
1-1/3 cups milk
1 can (14oz) chicken broth
¼ cup butter or margarine, melted
2/3 cup crushed saltine crackers
¾ cup cashew halves

In a greased 9"x13" baking dish, layer the first 6 ingredients in the order listed. In a bowl, combine the soups, milk and broth. Pour over the casserole in the baking dish. Cover and refrigerate overnight.
Remove casserole from refrigerator and let it come to room temperature, about 30 minutes. Toss butter and cracker crumbs, sprinkle over casserole. Top with cashews. Bake, uncovered, at 350°F for 35-40 minutes or until macaroni is tender.

*** Condensed cream of broccoli soup can be substituted.

Chicken and Rice Casserole Makes 6 servings.

Otherwise known as a meal to come home from Iraq for. I would like to thank everyone currently or formerly in the military for your service.

2 cans condensed cream of mushroom soup
1 can cream of celery soup
1 soup can of milk
2 cups water
1 cup regular rice
1 cup wild rice
2 lbs boneless, skinless chicken breasts and thighs
1 envelope onion soup mix

Heat oven to 350°F. In a bowl, combine the soups, milk and water. Add rice. Spread on the bottom of a greased 9"x13" baking dish. Push chicken pieces into soup mixture. Sprinkle onion soup mix on top. Cover tightly with foil. Bake for 2 hours without opening the oven door. Check to make sure rice is tender and chicken is cooked before serving. Serve warm.

Your talent is God's gift to you. What you do with it is your gift back to God. - Anonymous

(Pictured: Cheesy Chicken pg 71, Vegetable Casserole pg 64, Mom's Bean Salad pg 26, Can't Leave Alone Bars pg 109)

Cheesy Chicken   Makes 4 servings.

Makes 4 servings, but plan ahead to make more because it's really good chicken.

3 Tbsp butter, melted
1 cup crushed Cheese-it crackers, any flavor***
¼ tsp pepper
4 boneless, skinless chicken breast halves
1/3 cup sour cream

Heat oven to 375°F. Spoon 1 Tbsp butter into a 2 qt square dish. In a shallow dish, combine cracker crumbs and pepper. Place the sour cream in a bowl, dip chicken pieces in sour cream and then in cracker crumbs. Place in prepared dish. Drizzle butter on top. Bake for 30 minutes or until internal temperature of chicken reaches 170°F. Serve warm.

***Chicken-in-a-biscuit crackers are good on this chicken also.

Too often we underestimate the power of a touch, a smile, a kind word, a listening ear, an honest compliment, or the smallest act of caring, all of which have the potential to turn a life around. - Leo Buscaglia

Chicken Biscuit Bake

Makes 6-8 servings.

1 can condensed cream of chicken soup
2/3 cup mayonnaise
2-3 tsp Worcestershire sauce
4 cups cooked, cubed chicken
3 cups cooked broccoli, chopped
1 medium onion, chopped
1 cup shredded cheddar cheese
1 tube refrigerated biscuits
2 eggs
½ cup sour cream
2 tsp celery seed
1 tsp salt

Heat oven to 375°F. In a bowl, combine the soup, mayonnaise and Worcestershire sauce. Stir in chicken, broccoli and onion. Pour into a greased 9"x13" baking dish. Sprinkle with cheese. Cover and bake for 20 minutes. Separate biscuits, cut each in half or quarters. Arrange, cut side down over hot chicken mixture. In a bowl, combine eggs, sour cream, celery seed and salt. Pour over biscuits. Bake, uncovered 20 minutes longer or until biscuits are golden brown.

***** Don't overcrowd the biscuits or they will be gooey in the middle.

Chicken Sopa

Makes 6-8 servings.

My Mom used to make this when we were growing up, then I changed the recipe a little.

6 soft tortilla shells
2 cups cooked chicken, chopped
10-3/4oz can of cream of chicken soup
14oz can ro-tel tomatoes and chilies, drained
1/2 cup milk
1 cup ricotta cheese
¼ tsp garlic-pepper seasoning
2 cups shredded Mexican cheese blend
Parmesan cheese

In a large bowl, combine soup, chicken, ro-tel, milk and ricotta cheese. In a lightly greased 9"x13" baking pan, spoon a small amount of sauce on the bottom. Place 3 tortilla shells on the sauce. Layer half of the soup mixture on the shells, then half of the shredded cheese. Repeat layers, ending with cheese. Sprinkle parmesan cheese on top. Bake at 375°F for 30 minutes or until cheese is melted and casserole is hot.

Grandma Lemon's Sandwiches   Makes 6 servings.

A different kind of sandwich. Very tasty.

6 slices of bologna
6 slices Velveeta cheese
1/3-1/2 cup mayonnaise
2 Tbsp onion, minced
6 hot dog buns
2 sweet pickle midgets, drained

In a food processor, chop the pickles and onion. Add the bologna, Velveeta and mayonnaise, process until smooth. Spoon this mixture into the hot dog buns. Bake at 375°F, uncovered, for 20 minutes or until buns are crusty and filling is warm. This can be done in a toaster oven as well. Serve warm.

Chicken Stew over Biscuits

Makes 4-6 servings.

This is a great stick-to-your-ribs meal.

2 envelopes chicken gravy mix
2 cups water
¾ cup white wine or chicken broth
2 garlic cloves, minced
1 tsp parsley
2 chicken bouillon cubes
½ tsp pepper
5 medium carrots, cut in small chunks
1 large onion, cut into 8 wedges
3 lbs boneless, skinless chicken breasts or thighs
3 Tbsp all-purpose flour
1/3 cup cold water
6 biscuits (homemade, store bought, etc)

In a slow-cooker, combine the first 7 ingredients until blended. Add carrots, onion and chicken. Cover and cook on low 6-7 hours. Increase heat to high. In a small bowl, mix the flour and cold water until smooth, gradually stir into slow cooker. Cover and cook one hour. Stir to shred the chicken.

Bake or reheat biscuits. Place biscuits in a soup bowl and pour the stew on top. Serve warm.

Ground Beef Casserole

Makes 6-8 servings.

This recipe came from an Amish family in Indiana.

8oz package wide egg noodles, cooked and drained
1 lb hamburger
Salt and pepper to taste
10oz tomato sauce
1 cup cottage cheese
8oz cream cheese, softened
1/3 cup chopped green onion
2 Tbsp melted butter

Heat oven to 350°F. In a skillet, brown the hamburger, drain. Add tomato sauce, salt and pepper and heat through. In a bowl, combine cottage cheese, cream cheese and onion. Spread half of the cooked noodles on the bottom of greased 2qt casserole dish. Cover with cheese mixture. Add remaining noodles, pour melted butter on top. Spread the meat mixture on noodles. Bake for 30 minutes or until heated through. Serve warm.

Hamburgers with Vegetable Soup

Makes 4 servings.

Serve with mashed potatoes or noodles and warm bread for a cozy meal.

1 lb ground beef, turkey, venison or combination.
1 can Vegetable Beef soup
½ soup can of water

Form meat into 4 patties. Sprinkle with salt and pepper. Brown the patties in an electric skillet. When both sides are browned, drain off grease. Pour the soup and water over patties, scrapping the bottom of the skillet. Cover and simmer for 45 minutes, stirring occasionally. Turn the burgers over every 15 minutes. The soup will reduce and thicken. Serve warm.

We should look for someone to eat and drink with before looking for something to eat and drink. Epicurus

Herbed Chicken Fettuccini

Makes 4 servings.

1 tsp poultry seasoning
1 lb boneless, skinless chicken breasts, cut into 1" strips
2 Tbsp olive oil
4 Tbsp butter, divided
2/3 cup water
2 Tbsp teriyaki sauce
2 Tbsp onion soup mix
1 envelope savory herb and garlic soup mix, divided
8oz fettuccini noodles
2 Tbsp parmesan cheese
1 Tbsp Worcestershire Sauce

In a skillet, sauté chicken strips in oil and 2 Tbsp butter, sprinkle with poultry seasoning. Sauté 5 minutes or until chicken juices run clear. Add the water, teriyaki sauce, onion soup mix and 2 Tbsp savory herb and garlic soup mix. Bring to a boil. Reduce heat, cover and simmer for 15 minutes. Cook the fettuccini according to package directions, drain. Add to the chicken mixture. Add parmesan cheese, Worcestershire Sauce, remaining butter and remaining savory herb and garlic soup mix. Toss to coat. Serve warm.

May the road rise up to meet you. May the wind always be at your back. May the sun shine warm upon your face, and rains fall soft upon your fields. And until we meet again, May God hold you in the palm of His hand. An Old Irish Blessing

Honey Lime Grilled Chicken Makes 4 servings.

Yum! Avoid over-cooking this chicken. Serve with Savory Rice, if desired or Potato Salad, or Broccoli with Morney Sauce, or . . . . The options are endless.

½ cup honey
1/4 cup soy sauce
¼ cup lime juice
½ tsp minced garlic
1 pc sliced ginger root
4 boneless, skinless chicken breasts (or other pieces)

In a bowl, combine honey, soy sauce, lime juice, garlic and ginger. Stir well. Reserve 1/3 cup for basting on the grill. Add chicken and coat well. Cover bowl and chill for 30-45 minutes. (Or overnight, or while you are at work) Drain and discard marinade. Grill chicken 6-7 minutes on each side, or until internal temperature reaches 160°F, basting with reserved marinade. Serve immediately.

(Pictured: Maple Pecan Pork Chops pg 81, Corn Pudding pg 56, Green Beans with Chestnuts & Bacon pg 58, Oreo Ice Cream Dessert pg 137)

Maple Pecan Pork Chops

Makes 8 servings.

This recipe was created especially for our family in Vermont. ♡

½- 1 tsp red pepper flakes
1 tsp salt
1 cup Vermont maple syrup
2 Tbsp cornstarch
8 boneless pork chops, thick-cut
1 cup apple juice
½-3/4 cup pecan halves or pieces

Heat oven to 350°F. On a very hot grill, cook pork chops on both sides just long enough to leave grill marks and give the pork chops flavor. Remove from grill and place in a 9"x13" baking pan. In a bowl, combine remaining ingredients. Pour sauce over the pork chops. Bake, uncovered, 20 minutes. Turn chops over and bake 10-15 minutes longer or until pork chops are done and internal temperature reaches 160°F and sauce has thickened. Serve warm.

Love me when I least deserve it, because that is when I really need it.
- Swedish Proverb

(Pictured: Meatloaf Miniatures pg 83, Baked Beans pg 54, Sweet Potato Casserole pg 63, Microwave Pickles pg 157)

Meat Loaf Miniatures

Makes 18 meat loaves.

1-1/2 cups ketchup
1/3 cup packed brown sugar
2 eggs
4 tsp Worcestershire sauce
2-1/2 cups Crispix cereal, crushed (or Rice/Corn Chex)
3 tsp onion powder
½-1 tsp seasoned salt
½ tsp garlic powder
½ tsp pepper
3 lbs ground beef

Heat oven to 375°F. In a bowl, combine ketchup and brown sugar. In a separate large bowl combine 1/2 cup ketchup/brown sugar sauce, eggs, Worcestershire sauce, cereal and seasonings, mix well. Let stand 5 minutes. Add ground beef and mix well. Press meat mixture into 18 muffin cups. Bake 18-20 minutes. Drizzle the ketchup sauce on top and bake 10 minutes longer. Serve warm.

A little Consideration, a little Thought for Others, makes all the difference.
A. A. Milne (Winnie-The-Pooh)

(Pictured: Oven Fried Cod pg 85, Maple Glazed Carrots pg 59, Savory Rice pg 62)

Oven Fried Cod **Easy!**

Makes 4 servings.

This fish has such nice flavors. Experiment with different breads to find your favorite combination.

1 lb cod, cleaned, deboned
2 cups soft bread crumbs***
1/2 cup butter, melted
1 small onion, cut into rings- optional

Dry cod and cut into 3" pieces. Dip into 1/4 cup + 2 Tbsp melted butter, then into soft bread crumbs. Place in a 9"x13" baking pan that has 2 Tbsp melted butter in the bottom. Repeat until all the cod is breaded. Spread the onion rings on top of the cod. Pour any remaining butter over the top. Bake at 375°F for 20 minutes or until cod is cooked through and flaky.

*** Any kind of bread works for this- sandwich bread, rolls, bagels or a combination. I really enjoy the combination of white or Hawaiian rolls and a cheddar-dill bagel. Yum!

Pork and Sauerkraut **Easy!** Makes 6-8 servings.

I love coming home to the smell of this cooking, especially in the Fall. Serve with some heavy rye bread for a hearty meal.

½ cup onion, chopped
3 Tbsp brown sugar
16oz sauerkraut, drained
3 potatoes, quartered
2 small apples, peeled, cored, quartered
2 cups chicken broth
4 boneless pork chops
4 hot dogs

Combine the sauerkraut, apples and potatoes. Layer half of the sauerkraut mixture, the meat, then remaining sauerkraut mixture into a slow cooker. Pour the chicken broth over the top. Cover the slow cooker and cook on low 6-8 hours. Serve hot.

Pulled Pork

Makes 10-12 servings.

This is always a hit! My brother Tim gets the credit for the original recipe. He always smokes the pork instead of using a slow cooker.

6-8lb pork butt roast
1 can chicken or vegetable broth
RUB SEASONING MIX
BBQ SAUCE FOR PORK
Buns

Place the pork butt in a slow cooker. Sprinkle RUB SEASONING (pg 155) on top. Pour chicken broth around pork. Cover and cook on low 8 hours. Remove from heat and juice, shred meat while still hot, removing as much fat as possible. Place meat in a large saucepan, cover with BBQ SAUCE FOR PORK (pg 154) until it's the desired consistency. Heat through. Serve on toasted buns or use as a filling in the STUFFED HAND SANDWICH RECIPE (pg 90).

May love and laughter light your days, and warm your heart and home.
May good and faithful friends be yours, wherever you may roam.
May peace and plenty bless your world with joy that long endures.
May all life's passing seasons bring the best to you and yours.

                                                            - Irish Blessing

Quiche

Makes 5-6 servings.

Any meat, cheese, vegetable, etc that you desire can be used in a quiche. Leftover meats and veggies are great for quiche.

1 unbaked pie crust
½ lb bacon, cooked, drained, crumbled
½ cup sautéed or caramelized onions
1-1/2 cup shredded cheese, desired flavor
1 Tbsp flour
4 eggs
1-1/2 cup whipping cream
½ cup milk or half & half
½-1 tsp salt
Dash of Worcestershire sauce

Prepare pie crust and line bottom and sides of a large quiche dish or pie pan. Combine cheese, bacon and flour, layer onto pie crust, add onions. In a bowl, combine remaining ingredients, whisk to blend. Slowly pour the egg mixture over the meat and cheese in the pie crust. Bake at 350°F for 1 hour until firm and crust is browned. Serve warm.

Tip: Carefully place strips of aluminum foil on the edge of the pie crust for the 1st half hour of baking time so the edges don't burn.

Sausage Brunch Braid

Makes 6-8 servings.

Good as a meal or as an appetizer.

12oz pork sausage
½ cup chopped onion
¼ cup chopped celery
½ tsp garlic powder
3 oz cream cheese, softened
2 Tbsp chives
1 tsp parsley
8oz tube refrigerated crescent rolls
1 egg, lightly beaten

In a skillet, cook sausage, onion and celery until meat is no longer pink and vegetables are tender, drain. Add garlic powder, cream cheese, chives and parsley. Cook and stir over low heat until cream cheese is melted. Set aside and let cool. Unroll crescent dough on a greased baking sheet, pressing perforations together. Roll into a 12"x10" rectangle. Spoon sausage mixture onto dough and spread to within 3" of long sides and 1" of ends. On each long side, cut ¾" wide strips 3" towards center. Starting at one end, fold alternating strips at an angle, forming a braid. Brush dough with beaten egg. Bake at 350°F for 20-25 minutes or until golden brown.

Great opportunities to help others seldom come, but small ones surround us every day. - Sally Koch

Stuffed Hand Sandwiches

Makes 5 sandwiches.

Go crazy with these! Great for breakfast, lunch or dinner. Serve with appropriate condiments on the side.

1 loaf frozen bread dough or roll dough for a smaller sandwich, thawed
15 slices of ham or turkey deli meat ***
5 slices of cheese*** or string cheese

Heat oven to 375°F. Thaw dough and divide into 5 sections. Making 1 at a time, flatten dough into a circle. Roll up 3 slices of deli meat and 1 slice of cheese (cheese in the middle) and place on the dough. Bring the dough up around the meat and pinch edges to seal completely (or use a sandwich or calzone mold) so filling doesn't leak out while baking. Place on a cookie tray. Repeat until all ingredients are used. Bake for 13-17 minutes or until bread is golden brown. Serve warm.

***Filling Variations-
- Fill bread with leftover shredded meats, cooked veggies, cheese.
- Scramble a few eggs, wrap a ham slice around 2 spoonfuls of eggs and shredded cheese.
- Wrap a slice of ham and cheese around a shelled hard-boiled egg.
- Brown 1 lb ground beef with onions. Drain, stir in 4 Tbsp cream cheese, 1 Tbsp taco seasoning and ¼ cup strained salsa until melted. Let cool. Sprinkle shredded cheddar cheese on flattened dough, top with meat mixture. This makes 5 sandwiches.
- Corned beef or turkey and sauerkraut. With 1000 island dressing on the side.
- A small hamburger patty with grilled onion and cheese.
- Grilled and cooled brats or hot dogs.
- Pepperoni or sausage, mushrooms, onions and cheese. Any pizza ingredients will work. Serve with warm pizza sauce.

Swedish Meatballs

Makes 14 servings.

Great for a party! Skip the noodles & serve with a toothpick.

2 eggs, beaten
¼ cup ketchup
¾ cup dry bread crumbs
2 Tbsp parsley
2 Tbsp Worcestershire Sauce
1 tsp onion powder
1 tsp garlic powder
1 tsp pepper
½ tsp salt
½ tsp chili powder
2 lbs ground beef
1 lb ground pork
2 envelopes brown gravy mix
1 cup sour cream
Dash each of nutmeg and pepper
Hot cooked egg noodles

Heat oven to 400°F. In a large bowl, combine the first 10 ingredients. Crumble meat over mixture and mix well. Shape into 1" balls (or use small cookie scoop). Place on a greased, foil-lined baking sheet. Bake for 20 minutes or until no longer pink.

In a Dutch oven, prepare gravy according to package directions. Add meatballs, cover and cook for 10 minutes or until heated through. Remove from heat. Stir in sour cream, nutmeg and pepper. Serve over noodles.

How wonderful it is that nobody need wait a single moment before starting to improve the world.- Anne Frank

(Pictured: Scotch Eggs pg 93, Baked Beans pg 54, Vegetable Pizza pg 18)

As we light a path for others, we naturally light our own way.- Mary Anne Radmacher

Scotch Eggs

Makes 5 scotch eggs.

After the first time I made this I realized 5 scotch eggs would never be enough for my family. They loved them. And they are great for leftovers the next day if reheated in a toaster oven. These were better than the ones served at the Scottish Festival! We sometimes enjoy a cheese sauce poured on as well.

1 lb bulk pork sausage
Seasoned salt, Hickory salt or salt and pepper to taste
5 hard-boiled eggs, shells removed
1 egg lightly beaten
1 cup crushed cornflakes *****

Heat oven to 400°F. Line a baking sheet with aluminum foil. Divide the sausage into 5 portions. Wrap the sausage around the egg so no egg shows through, sprinkle with salt and pepper. Dip in beaten egg and then in cornflake crumbs. Place on baking sheet. Bake, uncovered, for 30 minutes or until meat is no longer pink, turning every 10 minutes.

***** Other things can be used like crushed crackers, cereal, potato chips, seasoned bread crumbs, etc.

TIP - The easiest way I have found to make Scotch Eggs is to first divide up the sausage. Using the palms of my hands I flatten the sausage, wrap the egg, and set aside until all eggs are wrapped. Using the wet hand/ dry hand method, I dip the wrapped egg in the beaten egg with my "wet" left hand, then roll in the crumbs with my "dry" right hand and place the finished egg on the baking sheet. Using this method keeps the crumbs out of the beaten egg and too much beaten egg out of the crumbs.

Taco- Filled Pasta Shells

Makes 4-6 servings.

Hot, medium or mild- it's your preference.

1 lb hamburger
1 envelope taco seasoning
4oz cream cheese, softened
12 jumbo pasta shells, cooked
¼ cup melted butter
1 cup salsa
1 cup taco sauce
2 cups shredded Mexican blend cheese
1-1/2 cups crushed Doritoes
1 cup sour cream
2-3 chopped green onions

In a large skillet, brown hamburger, drain. Add taco seasoning- prepared according to package directions. Add cream cheese, cover and simmer 5-10 minutes until melted. Transfer to a bowl, chill for one hour. Cook pasta shells until al dente', drain. Gently toss with melted butter.

Spoon cold meat filling into each shell (a spoon and your fingers work best for this process). Pour salsa into a greased 9" square pan. Place filled shells on salsa. Pour taco sauce over shells. Cover and bake at 350°F for 30 minutes. Uncover, sprinkle with cheese and Doritoes. Bake 15 minutes longer. Serve with sour cream and green onions.

(Pictured: (Above)Taco-Filled Pasta Shells pg 94, Honey French Dressing pg 155 (Below) Thai Tuna Burgers pg 96, Pea-Cheese Salad pg 27)

Thai Tuna Burgers

Makes 16 tuna burgers.

I found this recipe on a tuna label and adapted it to our taste. It's a nice alternative to hamburgers.

33oz light tuna, in water
1-1/4 cups bread crumbs
½ tsp Penzeys 4/S sea salt
½ tsp onion powder
1 tsp red pepper flakes, use more if you like it spicy
1-1/4 cups chopped peanuts
¼ cup chopped green onion
1 egg
1-1/4 cups mayonnaise
16 burger buns
Lettuce leaves, tomato slices, cheese slices, tarter sauce

Drain tuna. In a large mixing bowl combine tuna, bread crumbs, seasonings, peanuts and green onion, mix well. Stir in mayonnaise and egg until all ingredients are well combined. Form mixture into 16 patties. Chill patties 30 minutes for better cooking results, these can be crumbly. Cook burgers on a lightly greased skillet or griddle until lightly browned and heated through, turning once. Melt cheese slice on burger if desired. Serve on buns with lettuce, tomato, cheese slices, tarter sauce, etc.

The best and most beautiful things in the world cannot be seen or even touched. They must be felt with the heart.- Helen Keller

Thanksgiving Pie **Easy!**

Makes 4-6 servings.

---

3 cups prepared stuffing
2 cups cubed, cooked turkey
1 cup shredded Swiss cheese
3 eggs
½ cup milk
Salt & pepper to taste

Heat oven to 350°F. Press the stuffing onto the bottom and up the sides of a well-greased deep dish 9" pie pan. Top with turkey and cheese. Beat eggs, milk and salt & pepper together and pour over meat. Bake for 35-40 minutes or until a knife inserted near the center comes out clean. Let pie sit 5 minutes before serving. Serve with cranberry sauce if desired.

Yum-e-setti

Makes 6-8 servings.

This recipe came from an Amish family in Indiana.

1 lb hamburger
Salt and pepper to taste
1 cup chopped celery
1 can tomato soup
8oz package of wide egg noodles- cooked and drained
1 can cream of chicken soup
1 lb Velveeta, cubed

Heat oven to 300°F. Brown meat and celery, Drain. Add salt and pepper and tomato soup. Add chicken soup to the noodles. In a 2 qt greased casserole dish, layer the beef mixture and the noodle mixture. Cover with cubed Velveeta. Cover with foil and bake for 45 minutes. Uncover and bake for 15 minutes. Serve hot.

CAKES, BARS, BROWNIES AND COOKIES

(Pictured: (Above) Butter Pecan Pie Cupcakes pg 100,
(Below) Peanut Butter Topped Brownies pg 114)

Butter Pecan Pie Cupcakes

Makes 18-24 cupcakes depending on size.

These cupcakes are a lot of work but the finished product is so worth the effort!

Cupcakes:
1 Butter Pecan Cake mix
Oil, water and eggs according to package directions.

Pecan Pie Filling: (crustless)
1 cup corn syrup
3 eggs
1 cup sugar
2 Tbsp melted butter
1 tsp vanilla extract
2 Tbsp milk
1 cup coarsely chopped pecans

Honey Frosting:
2 Tbsp butter, softened
4 Tbsp cream cheese, softened
½ tsp vanilla extract
3 Tbsp honey
3-4 cups powdered sugar

Hershey's Caramel sauce (Ice cream topping)

Sugared Pecans:
2 Tbsp butter
½ cup chopped pecans
1/4 cup brown sugar

Preheat oven to 350°F. Grease a pie pan and prepare 24 muffin cups.

Pecan Pie Filling: In a mixing bowl, beat together filling ingredients except pecans until smooth. Stir in pecan pieces. Pour into prepared pie pan. Bake 30 minutes or until center is set. Allow pie to cool 10 minutes. Stir up the pie in the pie pan until it is the consistency of chunky pudding.

Cupcakes: In a mixing bowl, prepare the butter pecan cake according to the recipe on the box. Pour batter into muffin cups and bake according to the directions on the box.

Allow the cupcakes to cool completely on a wire rack. Gently cut a cone out of the top of the cupcake, set aside. Spoon the pecan pie filling into the cupcakes, just to the top of the cupcake. Replace half of each cut-out cone over the filling if desired.

Frosting: In a mixing bowl, beat together butter and cream cheese until well blended. Add vanilla, honey and 1 cup powdered sugar. Continue to add powdered sugar until desired consistency. Chill frosting for about 30 minutes. Frost cupcakes.

Sugared pecans: Melt butter in a saucepan, add brown sugar and pecan pieces. Cook on medium heat, stirring often, until sugar is dissolved and pecans are coated, about 10 minutes. Pour pecans out onto parchment paper and let cool. Break up pecans when cool.

Drizzle Caramel Sauce on top of cupcake. Sprinkle sugared pecans on top. Store in refrigerator.

Do you know your next door neighbor?- Mother Teresa

Caramel Chocolate Cake

Makes 16-20 servings.

1 package chocolate cake mix
Eggs, oil and water according to package directions
1 jar caramel topping
8oz frozen whipped topping, thawed
3 candy bars, coarsely crushed (Butterfinger, English Toffee bits, Reese's peanut butter cups, Skor Bar, etc)

Prepare and bake cake according to package directions in a greased 9" x 13" baking dish. Remove cake from oven when a toothpick inserted in the center comes out clean. Cool on a wire rack for 30 minutes. Poke 12 holes in the warm cake. Pour caramel topping over cake and in holes. Cool completely. Spread with whipped topping. Sprinkle with crushed candy bars. Chill 2 hours before serving. Store leftover cake in the refrigerator.

Chocolate Covered Cherry Cake   Makes 16-20 servings.

This recipe came from the Knoxville News Sentinel in the 80's. It's a very moist cake.

1 package Devil's Food cake mix
1 tsp. almond flavoring
2 eggs
1/3 cup water
1/3 cup oil
1 can cherry pie filling

Frosting:
1 cup sugar
5 Tbsp butter
1/3 cup evaporated milk
6oz semi-sweet chocolate chips
1 tsp vanilla

Heat oven to 350°F. In a mixing bowl, combine the first 5 ingredients. Fold in cherry pie filling. Pour batter into a greased and floured 9"x13" baking pan. Bake for 25-30 minutes or until indention left by your finger bounces back. Cool.

Frosting- Bring sugar, butter and milk to a boil; boil for one minute, stirring occasionally. Remove from heat and stir in chocolate chips until melted. Stir in vanilla. Pour over cake while still in pan. Let stand until cool.

Seize the moment. Think of all those women on the "Titanic" who waved off the dessert cart. Erma Bombeck

Chocolate Chip Cookie Dough Cupcakes

Makes 18-24 cupcakes.

Again, these cupcakes are a lot of work but the finished product is so worth the effort!

For the cupcakes:
1-1/2 cups butter, at room temperature
1-1/2 cups light brown sugar, packed
4 large eggs
1-1/3 cups pastry flour
1-1/3 cups flour
1 tsp baking powder
1 tsp baking soda
1/4 tsp salt
1 cup milk
2 tsp vanilla extract
1 cup mini semisweet chocolate chips

For the filling:
1/4 cup butter, at room temperature
6 Tbsp light brown sugar
1 cup plus 2 Tbsp flour
7 ounces sweetened condensed milk
1/2 tsp vanilla extract
1/4 cup mini semisweet chocolate chips

For the frosting:
1-1/2 cups butter, at room temperature
3/4 cup light brown sugar, packed
3-1/2 cups powdered sugar
1 cup flour
3/4 tsp salt
3 Tbsp milk
2-1/2 tsp vanilla extract

Preheat the oven to 350° F. Line cupcake pan with 24 liners. In a mixing bowl, combine the butter and brown sugar. Beat together until light and fluffy, about 3 minutes. Mix in the eggs one at a time, beating well after each addition. Combine the flour, baking powder, baking soda, and salt in a bowl. Add the dry ingredients to the mixer bowl, alternating with the milk, mixing each addition just until incorporated. Blend in the vanilla. Fold in the chocolate chips. Divide the batter evenly between the prepared cupcake liners. Bake for 18-20 minutes, until a toothpick inserted in the center comes out clean. Allow to cool in the pan 5-10 minutes, transfer to a wire rack to cool completely.

Cookie dough filling: Combine the butter and sugar in a mixing bowl and cream until light and fluffy, about 2 minutes. Beat in the flour, sweetened condensed milk and vanilla until smooth. Stir in the chocolate chips. Cover with plastic wrap and refrigerate until the mixture has firmed up, about a half hour.

To fill the cupcakes, cut a cone-shaped portion out of the center of each cupcake. Fill each hole with a chunk of the chilled cookie dough mixture.

Frosting: Beat together the butter and brown sugar in a mixing bowl until creamy. Mix in the powdered sugar until smooth. Beat in the flour and salt. Mix in the milk and vanilla extract until smooth and well blended. Chill frosting for 30 minutes or until firm enough to frost cupcakes. Frost the filled cupcakes and sprinkle with mini-chocolate chips.

Glazed Lemon Cake

Makes 16-20 servings.

So moist and delicate, with a nice lemon flavor.

1 box white cake mix
3.4oz instant lemon pudding mix
3 eggs
¾ cup vegetable oil
1 cup lemon-lime soda

Glaze:
1 cup powdered sugar
1/8 cup lemon juice

Heat oven to 350°F. In a mixing bowl, combine eggs and oil, Add cake mix and pudding mix and beat well. Stir in soda. Pour into a greased 9" x 13" baking dish. Bake 25-30 minutes or until cake bounces back when touched. Remove from oven, cool slightly.
In a bowl, mix powdered sugar and lemon juice until smooth. Pour glaze over warm cake. Cool.

Iced Pineapple Dump Cake

Makes 16-20 servings.

Although this is not the prettiest cake I have ever made, it gets compliments every time!

2 cups flour
1 tsp salt
1 tsp baking soda
1-1/2 cups sugar
2 eggs
20oz can crushed pineapple in juice, undrained
½ cup brown sugar
1 cup chopped pecans

Frosting:
½ cup evaporated milk
1 cup sugar
½ cup butter or margarine
1 tsp vanilla extract

Heat oven to 350°F. In a mixing bowl, combine the first 6 ingredients, mixing well. Pour into a greased 9" x 13" baking pan. Sprinkle brown sugar and pecans on top. Bake 25-30 minutes or until edges are lightly browned and center is done.
In a saucepan combine frosting ingredients. Cook until smooth and hot. Drizzle over warm cake.

There is no sight on earth more appealing than the sight of a woman making dinner for someone she loves. Thomas Wolfe

Yum Yum Cake

Makes 1 two-layered cake.

This is an easy cake to make, but everyone will think you slaved in a hot kitchen all day ☺ Every time I make it, someone asks for the recipe. Makes nice cupcakes too!

1 box yellow cake mix- not the butter kind
½ cup oil
3 eggs
1 can mandarin oranges, undrained (watch for seeds)

Frosting:
8 oz frozen whipped topping, thawed
1 large box instant vanilla pudding
20oz can crushed pineapple, undrained

Heat oven to 350°F. In a mixing bowl, combine oil, eggs and mandarin oranges. Add cake mix and beat until smooth. Pour batter into 2 greased and floured round cake pans. Bake for 25-30 minutes or until cake springs back when touched. Cool. Remove from pans.

Frosting- In a bowl combine pudding mix and pineapple until blended. Fold in whipped topping. Chill for 1 hour. Frost cake between the two layers and on top and sides of cake. Store in the refrigerator.

Can't Leave Alone Bars

Makes 20-24 bars.

Appropriate name for a delicious treat. These bars have the texture of a soft cookie with a creamy chocolate filling.

1 package white cake mix
2 eggs
1/3 cup vegetable oil
14oz can sweetened condensed milk
6oz semi-sweet chocolate chips
¼ cup butter or margarine

Heat oven to 350°F. In a bowl, combine cake mix, eggs and oil. With floured hands, press two-thirds of the mixture into a greased 9"x13" baking pan. In a microwave-safe bowl, combine the milk, chocolate chips and butter. Microwave 45 seconds, stir. Microwave 45-50 seconds longer or until chocolate chips and butter are melted, stir until smooth. Pour over crust in baking pan. Gently flatten pieces of the remaining cake mixture with your hands and lay on the chocolate layer. Bake for 20-25 minutes or until lightly browned. Cool before cutting.

Ginger Bars

Makes 20-24 servings.

These bars are also good with Sweet Caramel Glaze instead of the frosting.

1 cup butter or margarine
1 cup sugar
2 eggs
1 cup water
½ cup molasses
1-1/2 cups all purpose flour
1 cup pastry flour
1 tsp baking soda
1 tsp ground cinnamon
½ tsp ground cloves
½ tsp ground ginger
½ tsp salt

Frosting:
1/3 cup butter
1/4 teaspoon salt
1 teaspoon vanilla extract
½ tsp cinnamon
3-1/2 cups powdered sugar
3-4 Tbsp milk or light cream, enough to make smooth and spreadable.

Heat oven to 350°F. In a mixing bowl, cream butter and sugar. Add eggs, beat well. Add water and molasses, beat well. In a bowl, sift together the dry ingredients. Add to mixing bowl and mix well. Spread into a greased 15"x 10" x 1" baking pan. Bake 20-22 minutes or until bars test done, don't overbake. Cool.

Frosting:
Cream butter, salt, vanilla and cinnamon, beating with mixer until light and fluffy. Add the powdered sugar gradually, beating after each addition. Add 3 tablespoons milk or light cream, beating until smooth. Beat in more milk until desired spreading consistency is reached and the frosting is spreadable. Spread on cooled bars.

Sweet Caramel Glaze

2 cups powdered sugar
¼ cup butter or margarine, melted
2 tsp caramel syrup
1-2 tsp milk- enough to make it pourable

Combine the first 3 ingredients with a mixer. Mix in enough milk to make a glaze consistency. Pour and spread over almost cooled cake.

Oatmeal Breakfast Bars

Makes 20 squares.

Great for an on-the-go breakfast.

4 cups oats
1 cup brown sugar
1 tsp salt
1-1/2 cups chopped walnuts
1 cup coconut
¾ cup butter, melted
¾ cup orange marmalade or apple jelly.

Heat oven to 425°F. In a mixing bowl, combine all ingredients. Press evenly into a 9" x 13" cookie sheet. Bake 15-17 minutes or until golden brown, making sure the bottom doesn't burn. Cut into bars while warm.

Smores Bars

Makes 16-20 cookie bars.

Smores without a campfire! You can enjoy them all year long.

1/2 cup butter, room temperature
1/4 cup brown sugar
1/2 cup sugar
1 large egg
1 tsp vanilla extract
1-1/3 cups all purpose flour
3/4 cup graham cracker crumbs
1 tsp baking powder
1/4 tsp salt
7-8 Hershey's milk chocolate bars (enough to fit)
15 oz jar marshmallow creme

Preheat oven to 350°F. Grease a 9"x13" inch baking pan. In a mixing bowl, cream together butter and sugars until light. Beat in egg and vanilla. In a small bowl, whisk together flour, graham cracker crumbs, baking powder and salt. Add to butter mixture and mix at a low speed until combined. Divide dough in half and press half of dough into an even layer on the bottom of the prepared pan. Place chocolate bars over dough, break the chocolate (if necessary) to get it to fit in a single layer no more than 1/4 inch thick. Spread chocolate with marshmallow creme. Using floured hands, flatten remaining dough and lay on top of the fluff. Spread it around gently. Bake for 30 to 35 minutes, until lightly browned. Cool completely before cutting into bars.

One of the very nicest things about life is the way we must regularly stop whatever it is we are doing and devote our attention to eating. Luciano Pavarotti

Peanut Butter Topped Brownies   Makes 24 brownies.

How can you go wrong with chocolate and peanut butter? And all on top of a dense brownie. Sorry, I'm having a moment . . . .

Brownie Base
1 box (1 lb 6.5 oz) brownie mix
Water, vegetable oil and eggs called for on brownie package

Filling
1/2 cup butter, softened
3/4 cup creamy peanut butter
2 cups powdered sugar
2 teaspoons milk

Topping
1 cup semisweet chocolate chips
1/4 cup butter

Heat oven to 350°F. Grease bottom only of 9" x 13" baking pan. In a bowl, stir brownie mix, water, oil and eggs until well blended. Spread in pan. Bake 28 to 30 minutes or until toothpick inserted comes out almost clean. Cool completely, about 1 hour.

In a mixing bowl, beat filling ingredients until smooth. Spread mixture evenly over brownie base.

In small microwavable bowl, microwave topping ingredients on High 30 to 60 seconds; stir until smooth. Cool 10 minutes; spread over filling. Refrigerate about 30 minutes or until set. Cut into squares. Store covered in refrigerator.

Chocolate Coconut No-Bake Cookies

Makes 26-30 cookies.

½ cup chocolate chips
3-1/2 Tbsp butter or margarine, softened
8 large marshmallows
2 cups sugar
¼ cup cocoa
½ cup milk
½ cup peanut butter
4 to 4-1/2 cups quick oats
1 cup coconut
1 ½ tsp vanilla extract

In a saucepan melt the first 7 ingredients. Bring to a boil, and boil 1 minute. Remove from heat and stir in oats, coconut and vanilla. Drop by a large spoonful onto waxed paper to cool. Store in an air-tight container.

(Pictured: Oreo Pudding Cookies pg 116)

Oreo Pudding Cookies

Makes two dozen cookies.

These cookies are very moist and full of flavor.

1 cup butter, room temperature
3/4 cup brown sugar
1/4 cup white sugar
1 (4.2 ounce) package instant Oreo Pudding mix
1-1/2 cups all purpose flour
3/4 cup pastry flour
1 tsp baking soda
2 eggs
1 tsp vanilla
1/4 tsp salt
1 Hershey's Cookies-N-Cream King-Sized Candy Bar broken into small pieces
2 cups semi-sweet chocolate chips

Preheat oven to 350°F. Combine flours, baking soda, and salt in a small bowl and set aside. In a mixing bowl, cream together butter and sugars. Beat in pudding mix until blended. Add the eggs and vanilla and mix well. Add the flour mixture and mix to combine. Stir in cookies n' cream pieces and chocolate chips. Batter will be thick. Using a cookie dough scoop, place golf ball sized dough balls on a baking sheet lined with parchment paper. Bake for 10 minutes. You do not want to overbake these! Let cookies cool for 5 minutes on baking sheet before moving to a cooking rack. Store in air-tight container.

Wherever you go, go with all your heart.- Confucius

Peanut Butter Cookies

Makes 3 dozen cookies.

½ cup sugar
½ cup packed brown sugar
½ cup peanut butter
½ cup butter or margarine, softened
1 egg
1-1/4 cups flour
¾ tsp baking soda
½ tsp baking powder
¼ tsp salt

In a mixing bowl, beat together sugars, butter, peanut butter and egg. Sift the dry ingredients together and add to the mixing bowl. Beat well. Wrap dough in plastic wrap and chill 3 hours. Heat oven to 375°F. Shape dough into 36 balls and place on cookie sheets. Using a fork dipped in sugar, press down dough to make a crisscross pattern. Bake for 8-10 minutes or until cookies are light brown. Cool completely on a wire rack.

Snowy Butter Cookies

Makes about 3 dozen cookies.

My All-Time Favorite Cookie! Freezing them to make them last longer doesn't help, I have been known to eat them frozen.

1 cup butter, softened- no substitute
½ cup powdered sugar + more for baked cookies
½ tsp salt
1 cup finely chopped nuts
1 Tbsp vanilla extract
2 cups flour

Heat oven to 325°F. In a mixing bowl, cream butter, gradually beat in sugar and salt until light and fluffy. Add nuts and vanilla. Blend in flour. Shape into balls or crescents (moon shaped) using 1 Tbsp of dough each. Bake for 15-20 minutes, don't let cookies brown. Cool slightly, then roll in powdered sugar. Cool completely.

(Pictured: Chocolate Coconut No-Bake Cookies pg 115, Peanut Butter Cookies pg 117, Snowy Butter Cookies pg 118)

PIES AND DESSERTS

(Pictured: Chocolate Sundae Pie pg 122, Frozen Peanut Butter Pie pg 124 (Below) Grape Salad pg 134)

Apple Tarts

Makes 12 tarts.

2 apples- peeled, cored and chopped
1 can apple pie filling
1 cup sugar
Drizzle corn syrup- optional
1 Tbsp cinnamon
1/2 tsp nutmeg
1/8 tsp cloves
1 Tbsp brown sugar
2 premade pie crusts, unbaked- cut into 4-1/2" diameter circles

Topping:
1/8 cup flour
1/8 cup sugar
1/8 cup packed brown sugar
1/8 cup oats
1-2 Tbsp melted butter

Shape pie crust circles into lightly greased muffin cups to form tart shells. ***Bake at 400°F for 5 minutes.
In a saucepan combine all filling ingredients and cook until sauce thickens but apples are still firm. Spoon into tart shells. Combine topping ingredients in a small bowl until crumbly. Sprinkle on tarts and bake at 400°F for 20-25 minutes or until the crust is golden brown.

*** Prick the bottom of the crust with a fork. Place scrunched up aluminum foil balls into tarts to prevent them from losing the tart shape. Remove balls before filling tarts.

Blueberry Tarts

Makes 12 tarts.

1 cup sugar
¼ cup flour
½ tsp lemon peel- optional
Dash of salt
16oz blueberries
1/8 tsp cornstarch
2 tsp lemon juice
1 Tbsp butter
2 premade pie crusts, unbaked- cut into 4-1/2" diameter circles.

Shape pie crust circles into lightly greased muffin cups to form tart shells. ***Bake at 400°F for 5 minutes.
In a saucepan combine sugar, flour, lemon peel and salt. Add blueberries and cornstarch. Cook on medium heat until sauce is thickened and deep purple. Spoon filling into tart shells. In a small bowl, combine lemon juice and melted butter. Drizzle over the tarts. Bake at 400°F for 25-30 minutes or until the crust is golden brown.

*** Prick the bottom of the crust with a fork. Place scrunched up aluminum foil balls into tarts to prevent them from losing the tart shape. Remove balls before filling tarts.

Be careful of the words you say, keep them soft and sweet; You never know from day to day which ones you'll have to eat. Unknown

Chocolate Sundae Pie

Makes 6-8 servings.

This is easy dessert to keep in the freezer and pull out as needed. Not as sweet as most pies.

4oz cream cheese softened
½ cup sweetened condensed milk
4 tsp cocoa
8oz whipped topping, thawed
1 chocolate or graham cracker crumb crust or 6-8 individual graham cracker tart shells
½ cup chocolate syrup
½ cup chopped pecans

In a mixing bowl, beat cream cheese until smooth. Add milk and cocoa, beat well. Fold in whipped topping. Drizzle a little chocolate syrup in the bottom of the pie crust. Spoon filling into crust. Drizzle with chocolate syrup and pecan pieces. Cover and freeze overnight.

French Silk Pie

Makes 6-8 servings.

In High School I made this pie to flirt with cute boys! That's another thing Bekah inherited from me ♡♡ (see Frozen Peanut Butter Pie recipe)

3/4 cup butter, softened
1-1/8 cup sugar
1-1/2 tsp vanilla extract
3 eggs***
1-1/2 squares unsweetened chocolate, melted
9" baked pie crust

In a bowl, cream butter and sugar, beat well so it's not grainy. Add melted chocolate and vanilla. Beat in eggs, one at a time, beating 5 minutes after each one. Pour into the pie crust. Chill overnight.

***This recipe calls for raw eggs. Egg substitutes may be used, just watch the ingredients label because most brands add seasonings like onion and garlic powder which are good for quiche but would taste really bad in this pie.

Frozen Peanut Butter Pie Makes 6-8 servings.

"How to get the guy pie!" Bekah gets the credit for coming up with the original version of this pie which she made a lot of as a teenager 💕 *This makes a very full pie.*

8oz cream cheese, softened
1 can sweetened condensed milk
1 cup peanut butter
8 oz frozen whipped topping
7-8 Reese's candy bars- 3-4 quartered and 4 chopped up
1 Graham cracker or chocolate crust or 12-16 tart shells

In a mixing bowl, beat cream cheese until smooth, add milk and peanut butter. Fold in whipped topping and chopped candy bars. Spoon into the graham cracker crust. Garnish with a quarter of the candy bar. Freeze overnight. Serve frozen.

Banana Split Salad

Easy!

Makes 10 servings.

14oz sweetened condensed milk
12oz frozen whipped topping, thawed
1 can cherry pie filling
3 bananas, cut into chunks
8oz crushed pineapple, drained
½ cup chopped nuts

In a bowl, combine the milk and whipped topping until well blended. Fold in remaining ingredients. Chill until ready to serve.

Pumpkin Tarts

Makes 18-20 tarts.

3/4 cup granulated sugar
1 tsp ground cinnamon
1/2 tsp salt
1/2 tsp ground ginger
1/4 tsp ground cloves
1/2 tsp nutmeg
½ tsp pumpkin pie spice
2 large eggs
1 can (15 oz.) 100% Pure Pumpkin
1 can (12 fl. oz.) Evaporated Milk
3 unbaked pie crusts- cut into (18-20) 4-1/2" diameter circles.

Topping:
1 Tbsp butter, softened
½ cup powdered sugar
4oz cream cheese, softened
½ tsp vanilla extract
½ Tbsp milk
4oz frozen whipped topping, thawed
Cooled pumpkin filling

Heat oven to 350°F. Shape pie crust circles into lightly greased muffin cups to form tart shells *** Bake at 350°F for 5 minutes.

In a mixing bowl combine pie ingredients until well blended. Using a ladle, spoon filling into tart shells until it almost reaches the top of the crust. Bake for 25 minutes or until center is done and crusts are golden brown. Pour remaining pie filling into a pie pan and bake for approximately 25 minutes or until done in the center. This will be used in the topping. Cool.

Topping:

In a mixing bowl, combine butter and powdered sugar. Beat until creamy. Mix in vanilla, and milk. Add cream cheese, beat well until smooth. Stir in cooled pumpkin pie filling. Fold in whipped topping. Chill for 30 minutes. Spoon or pipe topping onto each cooled tart. Dust cinnamon on top if desired. Store in a sealed container in the refrigerator.

*** Prick the bottom of the crust with a fork. Place scrunched up aluminum foil balls into tarts to prevent them from losing the tart shape. Remove balls before filling tarts.

Remember, no matter where you go, there you are.- Confucius (I thought Grandpa Ching said this?)

(Pictured- (Above) Banana Split Salad pg 125, (Below) Apple Crisp pg 129)

Apple Crisp **Easy!**

Makes 8 servings.

Apple Crisp is an easy dessert to make and is a favorite treat any time of the year, not just in the Fall.

6-8 apples, peeled, cored and sliced
1/3- 1/2 cup sugar, depending on how sweet the apples are
1 tsp cinnamon
1-1/2 Tbsp butter

Topping:
½ cup flour
½ cup oats
½ cup sugar
½ cup brown sugar
1/3 cup butter or margarine

Heat oven to 375°F. Combine apples, sugar and cinnamon. Spread into a 9"x13" baking pan. Dot with butter.

Topping: Combine first 4 ingredients, cut in butter (I do this with my small food chopper). Sprinkle over apples. Bake 30 minutes or until apples are tender and topping is golden brown. Serve warm.

Anyone can cut an apple open and count the number of seeds. But, who can look at a single seed and count the trees and apples? *Dottie Walters*

Chocolate Chip Cheese Ball

Makes 1 cheese ball.

I know this sounds a little odd but try it please. Once you make it and share it, it will be a much- requested dessert.

8oz cream cheese, softened
½ cup butter (no substitutes)
¼ tsp vanilla extract
¼ tsp almond extract
¾ cup powdered sugar
2 Tbsp brown sugar
1/3 cup chopped maraschino cherries- optional
¾ cup mini semisweet chocolate chips
¾ cup finely chopped pecans
Graham crackers or animal crackers

In a bowl, combine cream cheese, butter, vanilla and almond extract until fluffy. Gradually add brown sugar and powdered sugar, beat until just combined. Stir in chopped cherries and chocolate chips. Cover and chill for 2 hours. Shape mixture into a ball or disk, wrap tightly with plastic wrap, chill 1 hour. Roll ball in chopped pecans and serve with graham crackers.

Variations: Combine chopped, toasted pecans and toasted coconut and roll the cheese ball in this.

The best way to find yourself, is to lose yourself in the service of others. - Ghandi

Frozen Banana Jungle Treats

Makes 12-14 halves.

This is a simple recipe from Home Ec. class in High School. Nice summer-time treat.

6oz butterscotch chips
½ cup peanut butter
3-5 cups crushed Life cereal
6-8 bananas, cut in half or in thirds for a bite- sized treat

Melt the butterscotch chips and peanut butter in a double boiler. Cook until melted and well blended. Spread a large piece of wax paper on a cookie sheet. Remove mixture from heat. Dip bananas in mixture, shaking off excess and roll into crushed cereal. Place on wax paper. When all bananas are done, place pan in the freezer. Once frozen, the bananas can be stored in a container or bag in the freezer. Eat frozen- once thawed the bananas get mushy.

Fruit Salad

Makes 4-6 servings.

6oz carton of yogurt- any flavor
3/4 cup strawberries, sliced
2 apples, peeled, cored and chopped
1 banana, sliced
½ cup grapes, halved
1/4 cup maraschino cherries, chopped
1/2 cup miniature marshmallows- optional
½ cup chopped nuts- optional
½ cup granola- optional

Mix all ingredients and chill until ready to serve.

Fruit Slush

Makes 10-12 servings.

Gabrielle's favorite treat ♡

2 cups boiling water
2 cups sugar
12oz orange juice
20oz crushed pineapple in juice
2 bananas
6oz chopped maraschino cherries
4 cups Sprite

This will increase in size as it freezes so make it in a large bowl. Dissolve sugar in hot water. Stir in remaining ingredients. Cover and store in the freezer, stirring every couple hours until frozen. Remove from freezer before serving to make it a slushy consistency.

Grape Salad

Makes 8 servings.

Karl's Favorite- odd really, considering he doesn't care much for grapes.

2-1/2 to 3 lbs red and green grapes, washed & dried thoroughly
8oz cream cheese, softened
8oz sour cream
½ cup brown sugar
1 tsp vanilla

Topping:
½ cup brown sugar
½ cup chopped pecans

In a mixing bowl, combine the cream cheese, sour cream, brown sugar and vanilla. Fold in grapes. Cover and store in the refrigerator overnight. Stir salad before adding the topping at serving time.

In a small bowl, combine the brown sugar and pecans for the topping. Sprinkle on top of the salad. Serve chilled.

Tang Dessert Make 6-8 serving.

Yes Tang- the drink mix! There will be a little leftover filling, good for a tart or two.

1 pint sour cream
1 can sweetened condensed milk
8oz whipped topping, thawed
½ cup Tang (dry drink mix)
1 large graham cracker crust or 6-8 tart shells

In a mixing bowl, combine the first 4 ingredients. Spoon into the graham cracker crust. Cover and store in the freezer overnight.

Mom's Cinnamon Jell-O   Makes 8 servings.

This is an annual Christmas treat at our house.

1 large box cherry Jell-o
2 cups boiling water
1 cup applesauce
1 cup red hots
Frozen whipped topping, thawed

In a saucepan, melt the red hots in the boiling water. Remove from heat, stir in jello mix. When jello is dissolved, add applesauce. Pour into a 1-1/2 qt jello mold or bowl and chill overnight. Unmold onto a serving plate. Garnish with whipped topping and additional red hots if desired.

Oreo Ice Cream Dessert Makes 8 servings.

This recipe was a favorite dessert from childhood created by Kymme, who is way too young to be my Aunt! Thanks for teaching me about Nestle' Quik and Little Brown Koko

½ lb Oreo cookies, crushed, leaving some chunks
½ gallon vanilla ice cream

Mix the ice cream and Oreos, folding together until blended. Place in a loaf pan, cover and freeze until hard. Slice and serve. Store in the freezer.

Variations-
To this recipe add ½ cup chopped maraschino cherries, ¼ cup maraschino cherry juice and 1 tsp almond extract, mix as directed above.

Peanut Butter Apple Dessert

Makes 16 servings.

A simple but impressive layered dessert.

1-1/2 cups graham cracker crumbs
½ cup packed brown sugar
½ cup plus 1/3 cup peanut butter, divided
¼ cup butter or margarine, melted
8oz cream cheese, softened
¾ cup sugar
16oz frozen whipped topping, thawed
2 cans (21oz each) apple pie filling
¾ cup powdered sugar
1 tsp cinnamon

In a bowl, combine graham cracker crumbs, brown sugar, ½ cup peanut butter and butter. Spoon half into a 3 qt bowl or serving dish. In a mixing bowl, beat cream cheese and sugar until smooth, fold in whipped topping. Spread half over crumb mixture in bowl. Top with one can of apple pie filling. Combine powdered sugar, 1/3 cup peanut butter and cinnamon until crumbly. Sprinkle half on pie filling. Repeat layers. Chill until ready to serve.

Peanut Butter Chocolate Dessert   Makes 12 servings.

I make this often with other kinds of cookies- duplex, chocolate sandwich cookies, nutter butters, oreos, etc. You can change the flavor of cookie and pudding mix to whatever you want. It makes a great dirt pudding also, with gummy worms tucked into the pudding and crushed chocolate cookies.

2-1/4 cups crushed peanut butter cookies
¼ cup sugar
¼ cup melted butter
6oz cream cheese, softened
1 cup powdered sugar
12oz frozen whipped topping, thawed, divided
2-1/2 cups cold milk
2 packages (3.9oz each) instant chocolate pudding mix
Additional crumbled peanut butter or chocolate cookies

In a bowl, combine crushed cookies, sugar and butter, Press into an ungreased 9"x13" baking dish. Bake at 350°F for 6-8 minutes. Cool.

    In a mixing bowl, beat cream cheese and powdered sugar, fold in 1 cup whipped topping. Spread over cooled crust. In a mixing bowl, beat milk and pudding mix for 2 minutes or until thickened. Spread over cream cheese layer. Top with remaining whipped topping, sprinkle with crumbled cookies. Chill at least 1 hour before serving.

Tropical Ambrosia Makes 6 servings.

20oz can crushed pineapple, undrained
3.4oz package instant coconut cream pudding mix
8oz frozen whipped topping, thawed
½ cup flaked coconut, toasted
Maraschino cherries on stems, optional

Drain pineapple into a mixing bowl. Combine juice and pudding mix, beating about 2 minutes until thickened. Fold in whipped topping and pineapple. Transfer to a serving bowl. Top with Maraschino cherries and toasted coconut. Chill until ready to serve.

The Trifle:

There are planned trifles- with an actual recipe- and there are unplanned trifles- that use up bits and pieces, leftovers. Both are delicious. I tend to have small amounts of ingredients in the refrigerator, freezer or pantry that need to get used up like pieces of cake, cookies, whipped topping, chocolate chips, etc. Some of my best unplanned trifles have come from a "clean-out-the fridge, freezer and pantry" day.

Banana Trifle- Unplanned Trifle

Crumbled banana bread
Vanilla pudding
Banana slices
Nilla wafers
Frozen whipped topping, thawed
Caramel ice cream topping
Toffee pecans, crushed

Layer all ingredients in a trifle bowl or glass baking dish. Chill until ready to serve.

Lemon Trifle- Planned Trifle

Makes 10-12 servings.

1 large box lemon jello
1 large box instant lemon pudding
1 can Lemon Pie Filling
2 cups crushed sugar or lemon cookies
2 cups leftover cake, donuts, muffins, etc
12oz whipped topping
4 oz cream cheese, softened
½ cup powdered sugar
1 cup marshmallow crème
1 lemon- juice, zest and pulp if desired. Use part of the lemon as garnish
Blueberries as garnish

In a small bowl, dissolve jello in 1-1/2 cups boiling water. Add ½ cup cold water and set aside to thicken. In a small bowl, combine pudding mix and 2-1/4 cups cold milk. Set aside to thicken. In a mixing bowl, beat cream cheese until smooth. Add the powdered sugar, marshmallow crème, 2 cups cake, and juice, pulp and zest from the lemon, mixing well. Set aside.
To assemble trifle: Mix the thickening jello and 1-1/2 cups cookie crumbs. Spoon into a large trifle, serving bowl or 9"x13" glass dish. Chill 5-10 minutes. Spread on a layer of whipped topping, chill. Spread on the lemon pudding, chill. Spread on the cream cheese/cake filling, chill. Spread on the Lemon Pie Filling, chill. Spread on a layer of whipped topping. Sprinkle remaining ½ cup cookie crumbs on top. Garnish the top with lemon wedges or slices and blueberries if desired.

(Pictured: Lemon Trifle pg 142)

Dixie Peanut Brittle

Makes about 1 lb of brittle.

1-1/2 cups Spanish peanuts***
1 cup sugar
½ cup light corn syrup
1/8 tsp. salt
1 tsp butter
1 tsp vanilla extract
1 tsp baking soda

In a 2 qt microwave-safe bowl, combine the nuts, sugar, corn syrup and salt. Stir well. Microwave on high for 4 minutes. Stir in butter and vanilla. Stir well. Microwave an additional 4 minutes. Add baking soda quickly and stir until light and foamy (the mixture will increase in volume). Immediately pour onto a lightly greased baking sheet, spread to ¼" thickness. When cool, break into pieces. Store in an airtight container.

*** Use desired nuts. I like cashews, pecans, etc. Different nuts gives the brittle a different taste.

DRINKS

(Pictured: Strawberry Banana Smoothie pg 151,
Chocolate Coconut Martini pg 147)

Caramel Apple Martini

Easy!

Makes 2 martinis.

Since I liked the Chocolate Coconut Martini so much, I started experimenting with other flavors.

1 packet apple cider mix
2oz hot water
1oz cold water
1oz caramel syrup
2oz vodka
2oz Sour Apple Pucker
8 large pieces of ice
Splash of 7up or Sprite as garnish
Cinnamon stick for garnish if desired

Dissolve the apple cider mix in the hot water. Pour into a martini shaker with remaining ingredients except 7up. Shake until well mixed. Pour into 2 martini glasses, garnish with 7up and cinnamon sticks.

Chocolate Coconut Martini   Makes 2 martinis.

I never thought I would like a martini until I made this.

1 package hot chocolate drink mix
2 oz hot water
1 oz cold water
3 oz coconut cream or syrup
3 oz whipped cream
4 oz vodka
Ice- About 8 large pieces
Shaved chocolate candy bar for garnish
Flaked coconut for garnish

Dissolve the hot chocolate mix in the hot water. Pour into a martini shaker with remaining ingredients. Shake until well mixed. Pour into 2 martini glasses, garnish with shaved chocolate and coconut.

Lemonade

Makes about a gallon.

This is a strong lemonade, serve with lots of ice.

2-1/2 cups Country Time Lemonade mix
1 cup sugar
¼ cup corn syrup
½ cup lemon juice (3 lemons)
Lemon zest and pulp (3 lemons)
Ice

In a large saucepan, combine Country Time, sugar, corn syrup and lemon juice. Boil until sugar is dissolved. Slowly add 2 cups water to the pan and stir until combined. Pour into a pitcher of ice. Add lemon zest and pulp and stir until ice is melted. Garnish with a lemon twist or wedge.

The unselfish effort to bring cheer to others will be the beginning of a happier life for ourselves. - Helen Keller

Mom's Eggnog

Makes about 4 cups.

4 cups milk (or combination of milk and half & half)
4 eggs or ½ cup egg substitute***
½ cup sugar
1 tsp vanilla
Nutmeg

Pour all ingredients into a blender and mix until smooth. Refrigerate until ready to serve. Sprinkle nutmeg on top if desired.

*** Egg-Beaters or egg substitute can be used for this if you can find some with no extra ingredients like onion powder, spices, etc. Check labels carefully.

Orange-Pineapple Punch

Makes 1 large punch bowl full.

12oz frozen orange juice concentrate
1 large can of pineapple juice
2 liter of Sprite, 7up or Gingerale
1 tub of Rainbow Sherbet

In a punchbowl, combine the orange juice concentrate and pineapple juice. Fill the empty OJ container twice with water and add to punch. Stir well. Pour in the Sprite. Just before serving, spoon in the frozen sherbet.

Variations:
Add orange or pineapple slices or maraschino cherries to punch.

For Smoothies:
Pour all ingredients into a blender. Process on high speed until all the ice is crushed and the drink is smooth.

Pina Colada Smoothie

Makes 2 servings.

---

1 banana
8oz can crushed pineapple with juice
½ cup liquid Pina Colada mix
½ cup orange sherbet
2 cups ice

Strawberry Banana Smoothies-1

Makes 2 servings.

8oz frozen strawberries (not in syrup)
1 banana
1 cup pineapple juice
2 Tbsp coconut cream
¼ cup grenadine
1 cup ice

Strawberry Banana Smoothies-2

Makes 2 servings.

---

8 frozen strawberries
2 bananas
8oz yogurt (desired flavor)
2 Tbsp strawberry jam
8-10 ice cubes

MISCELLANEOUS

(Pictured- Microwave Pickles pg 157)

After the game, the king and the pawn go into the same box. Italian Proverb

Barbeque Sauce for Pork

This makes 8-9 cups of BBQ sauce.

5 tsp hot sauce
1 cup vinegar
1/2 cup mustard
½ cup Rub Seasoning Mix
1 cup Worcestershire sauce
½ bottle of molasses
3 Tbsp lemon juice
1 cup brown sugar
8 cups ketchup
½ bottle of liquid smoke.

In a Dutch oven, mix hot sauce, vinegar, mustard and rub. Cook on medium heat until well combined. Add remaining ingredients, cover the Dutch oven and boil until sauce becomes red-brown in color, 10-20 minutes, stirring often so it doesn't burn on the bottom. Use this sauce with pulled pork or other pork recipes. Store in the refrigerator, freezer or can the sauce. A 9-10lb pork butt will require most of this BBQ sauce.

Rub Seasoning Mix

3 cups paprika
½ cup pepper
½ cup salt
1 cup sugar
2 Tbsp chili powder
½ cup garlic powder
½ cup onion powder

Mix all ingredients and store in pantry. Use to flavor meat or in sauces.

Honey French Dressing Makes 1-1/2 to 2 cups.

½ cup ketchup
½ cup vegetable oil
2 Tbsp apple cider vinegar
¼-1/2 cup honey- to taste
1 clove garlic, minced
¼ tsp salt
Dash of pepper
Dash of Worcestershire sauce

Combine all ingredients in a blender until smooth. Pour into a container and chill until ready to use. Store in the refrigerator.

Italian Salad Dressing Makes 1-1/2 cups dressing.

Very similar to the salad dressing from a popular Italian Restaurant.

½ cup white vinegar
1/3 cup water
1/3 cup vegetable oil
¼ cup corn syrup
2-1/2 Tbsp grated Romano cheese
2 Tbsp dry pectin (for jelly making)
2 Tbsp beaten egg- (1 small egg) or egg substitute
1-1/4 tsp salt
1 tsp lemon juice
½ tsp minced garlic
¼ tsp parsley flakes
Pinch of oregano
Pinch of crushed red pepper flakes

Combine all ingredients in a blender for 30 seconds. Chill at least one hour.

Microwave Pickles

Makes 4-6 servings.

Different vinegars produce different tasting pickles. I like apple cider vinegar for these pickles. I have also used cinnamon, cloves and nutmeg for a different taste.

2 medium cucumber, thinly sliced
½- 1 small onion, thinly sliced
¾ cup sugar
1/3 to ½ cup vinegar***
1 tsp salt
½ tsp celery seed

In a large microwave- safe bowl, combine all ingredients. Microwave on high 4 minutes, stir. Microwave 3-4 minutes longer or until mixture is bubbly and cucumber and onions are crisp-tender. Cover and chill at least 4 hours.

Lemon Curd

Makes 2-1/2 cups of Lemon Curd.

Tasty on an English muffin, toast, pancakes, etc.

4 large eggs
1-1/2 cups sugar
2 Tbsp lemon peel, chopped
Dash of salt
¼ cup butter, at room temperature
½ cup lemon juice

Beat eggs in a saucepan over a double boiler. Stir in remaining ingredients and cook over simmering water about 30 minutes until sauce is thick and smooth, stirring constantly (or you will get scrambled egg pieces). The sauce will thicken more as it cools. Cover and chill until sauce is cold. Spoon into a container, cover and store in the refrigerator. This will keep 2-3 weeks in the refrigerator.

Name Of Recipe	Page #
Apple Crisp	129
Apple Tarts	120
Bacon & Potato Soup	31
Baked Beans	54
Baked Cinnamon Brie Tart With Apple Pecan Sauce	11
Baked Cream Cheese Appetizer	12
Banana Bread	40
Banana Split Salad	125
Banana Trifle	141
BBQ Chestnuts	10
BBQ Sauce for Pork	154
Beef Stew with Mostaccioli	32
Blueberry Tarts	121
Broccoli Ham Casserole	67
Broccoli Salad	22
Broccoli with Morney Sauce	55
Butter Pecan Pie Cupcakes	100
Can't Leave Alone Bars	109
Caramel Apple Martini	146
Caramel Chocolate Cake	102
Cashew Chicken Casserole	68
Cheddar Ham Spread	13
Cheese Crisps	14
Cheese Fondue	15
Cheesy Chicken	71
Cheesy Garlic Bread	41
Chicken & Cheese Chowder	35
Chicken and Rice Casserole	69
Chicken Biscuit Bake	72
Chicken Salad	23
Chicken Sopa	73
Chicken Stew Over Biscuits	75
Chocolate Chip Cheese Ball	130

Name Of Recipe	Page #
Chocolate Chip Cookie Dough Cupcakes	104
Chocolate Coconut Martini	147
Chocolate Coconut No-Bake Cookies	115
Chocolate Covered Cherry Cake	103
Chocolate Sundae Pie	122
Cinnamon Crescent Rolls	42
Coffeecake with Cream Cheese Swirl	43
Corn Pudding	56
Creamy Italian Noodles	57
Dixie Peanut Brittle	144
Easy Beef Noodle Soup	33
French Silk Pie	123
Frozen Banana Jungle Treats	131
Frozen Peanut Butter Pie	124
Fruit Salad	132
Fruit Slush	133
German-Style Potato Salad	25
Ginger Bars	110
Glazed Lemon Cake	106
Grandma Lemon's Coffeecake	44
Grandma Lemon's Sandwiches	74
Grape Salad	134
Green Beans with Bacon & Chestnuts	58
Ground Beef Casserole	76
Hamburgers with Vegetable Soup	77
Herbed Chicken Fettuccini	78
Honey French Dressing	155
Honey-Lime Grilled Chicken	79
Iced Pineapple Dump Cake	107

Name Of Recipe	Page #	Name Of Recipe	Page #
Italian Salad Dressing	156	Potato Salad	28
Lemonade	148	Pulled Pork	87
Lemon Curd	158	Pumpkin Tarts	126
Lemon Trifle	142	Quiche	88
Maple Glazed Carrots	59	Ranch Pretzels	17
Maple Pecan Pork Chops	81	Rub Seasoning Mix	155
Meat Loaf Miniatures	83	Saucy Potatoes	61
Microwave Pickles	157	Sausage Brunch Braid	89
Mom's Bean Salad	26	Savory Rice	62
Mom's Cinnamon Jell-O	136	Scotch Eggs	93
Mom's Eggnog	149	S'Mores Bars	113
Mom's Rhubarb Bread	45	Snowy Butter Cookies	118
My Favorite Cornbread	46	Spicy Ranch Salad With Chicken	29
Oatmeal Breakfast Bars	112	Strawberry Banana Smoothies	152
Orange- Pineapple Punch	150	Stuffed Hand Sandwiches	90
Oreo Ice Cream Dessert	137	Swedish Meatballs	91
Oreo Pudding Cookies	116	Sweet Caramel Glaze	111
Oriental Chicken Salad	24	Sweet Coleslaw	30
Oven Fried Cod	85	Sweet Potato Casserole	63
Oven Fried Zucchini Circles	60	Sweet Tropical Bread	50
Pancakes	48	Taco- Filled Pasta Shells	94
Parmesan Rounds	16	Tang Dessert	135
Pea-Cheese Salad	27	Thai Tuna Burgers	96
Peanut Butter Apple Dessert	138	Thanksgiving Pie	97
Peanut Butter Chocolate Dessert	139	Tortellini & Sausage Stew	37
		Tropical Ambrosia	140
Peanut Butter Cookies	117	V-8 Cheese Loaves	51
Peanut Butter Topped Brownies	114	Vegetable Casserole	64
		Vegetable Pizza	18
Pina Colada Smoothies	151	Vegetable Sticks	19
Pizza Bread	49	Yum Yum Cake	108
Pork & Sauerkraut	86	Yumi-setti	98